53 SOUL-WINNING SERMON OUTLINES ON FIRST CORINTHIANS

BOOKS IN THE BIBLE STUDY TEXTBOOK SERIES:

- ACTS MADE ACTUAL
- SACRED HISTORY AND GEOGRAPHY
- THE CHURCH IN THE BIBLE
- ROMANS REALIZED
- HELPS FROM HEBREWS
- THE GLORIOUS CHURCH OF EPHESIANS
- THE GOSPEL OF JOHN VOL. I
- GUIDANCE FROM GALATIANS
- THE GREATEST WORK IN THE WORLD
- PAUL'S LETTERS TO TIMOTHY AND TITUS
- SURVEY COURSE IN CHRISTIAN DOCTRINE VOL. I
- SURVEY COURSE IN CHRISTIAN DOCTRINE VOL. II
- LETTERS FROM PETER
- THINKING THROUGH THESSALONIANS
- STUDIES IN FIRST CORINTHIANS
- THE SEER, THE SAVIOUR, AND THE SAVED IN THE BOOK OF REVELATION

53 SOUL-WINNING SERMON OUTLINES ON FIRST CORINTHIANS

by

Archie Word

COLLEGE PRESS, Joplin, Missouri

CONTENTS

Page

Page

"EVERY PREACHER'S GREAT DESIRE"

I Corinthians 1:1-3

Every true preacher has the desire, deep down in his heart, to some day establish a church where there is no church nearby. Paul set us the example by the many mission stations which he established on his three "world wide" mission tours. Naturally, the question as to what variety of church should be built comes to our mind when we contemplate establishing a new congregation. Here the Holy Spirit records the aspirations Paul had when he began the work in Corinth and sought to bring it to perfection.

PROPOSITION: *What sort of a church did Paul seek to build?*

I. IT WAS A CHURCH BUILT UPON CHRIST. I Cor. 1:1-3
- A. Paul said he laid the foundation. I Cor. 3:10
  In Rom. 15:20 he has said he did not want to build it on another man's foundation.
- B. He realized that no other foundation would be sufficient. I Cor. 3:11; Any other foundation is sand.
- C. He sought to build it out of material that would stand the fire test. I Cor. 3:12-15
  Possibly Paul knew the inclination of men to want to build rapidly for show, instead of slowly for longevity.

II. IT WAS BUILT OUT OF SAVED SINNERS. Romans 6:15-19
- A. Corinth was one of the wickedest, sinfullest cities in the Roman empire at that time. I Cor. 3:1 "Carnal"
  1. Paul did not hesitate to recall to saved people the condition they had been in, formerly. Eph. 4:22
  2. Paul knew in what condition all men find themselves. Romans 7:15-24

III. IT WAS A CHURCH STRIVING UNTO PERFECTION. Heb. 6:1
- A. That was the reason for his correcting them. I Cor. 1:10
  1. He urged them to leave all human philosophies. I Cor. 1:10
  2. He pleaded with them to be ONE UNITED BODY. 3:1-9
  3. It was to correct them that he sent Timothy. 4:17-21
  4. Immorality was exposed and condemned. 5:1-13

5. Proper relationship in marriage was stressed. (Chp. 7)
6. Thoughtfulness for others weaknesses was needed in order to grow up in Christ. (Chp. 8)
7. He instructed them in the support of their Minister. (Chp. 9)
8. He reminded them of the importance of proper observance of the Communion with Christ. (Chap. 11)
9. He gave new meaning to the word love, and admonished them as to its proper place in their lives. 14:1; 8:3

IV. IT WAS BUILT ON THE HOPE OF THE RESURRECTION.

A. This was the culminating act of the Gospel message. 15:4
B. This was what gave distinction to his message. Acts 17:32
C. This was his appeal, even to the philosophers. Acts 17:30-31
D. Because of this, he considered to die, gain. Phil. 1:21
E. This blessed hope sustained him in his own death. II Timothy 4:6-8

This is the type of church the Apostle sought to build whereever he went on his world tours preaching Christ. The churches then were so different from the churches now. Let us carefully discern the difference.

Radford once said, "Learning to discern differences is the fundamental work of all education. The child masters the alphabet by noting the difference in letters and their sounds. Soon he masters biology by noting the difference in shapes of organisms. Immortal painters are made by their ability to see and produce varying shades and tints of colors which others do not see. Beethovens are those who can detect a tune that is 99% perfect." Let us build, after the Divine order, His church as laid out in the epistles of the Apostles.

"CHECKING UP ON A MAN OF GOD"

I Cor. 1:1-2 cf. Acts 18:1-4

INTRODUCTION:

All successful business men make an inventory of their businesses at least once a year. Wiser men in business check up almost every day, especially in smaller works. Navigators check the progress of the ship on every shift. The man at the wheel never takes his eyes off the compass as his orders come to him from the "flying bridge." Steam gauges are for the purpose of checking the pressure in the boiler. Oil gauges, or "Red lights" on the car panel, are for checking the mechanical condition of your car. Thermometers inform the nurses as to the condition of the patient as they come around regularly in the hospital. All of these remind us that we need to check up on ourselves. We can learn from checking up on the lives of successful men of God who have gone on before.

PROPOSITION: *Let us check Paul on four points.*

I. WHAT TYPE OF COMPANY DID HE CHOOSE WHEN HE CAME TO CORINTH? Acts 18:1-2
   A. They were people of his own trade; they were Christians.
      1. They were of a congenial temperament. We do not know where nor when they were converted, but they were.
   B. They proved to be true and steadfast friends to Paul.
      1. They were parental instructors of Apollos. Acts 18:24-26
      2. They kept house in Ephesus, where Paul abode. Acts 18:32
      3. In Rome they had a church in their house. Rom. 16:3-5
   C. The variety of associates we form when we move into a new place, will largely tell what we are like inside, and it will largely determine our destiny. I Cor. 15:33

II. NOTICE WHERE PAUL FIRST WENT, AS HE ENTERED THE CITY. Acts 18:4
   A. He did not go to the theatre, TV store, cabaret, race track, or the Isthmian games.
   B. Where DID he go?
      1. He went to the house of God; the synagogue.
         He knew it was open on the Sabbath. Paul knew the worldly places of amusement were open too, yet he chose the better place to go.
      2. He went to the Jews first. They had a background knowledge of the prophets.
      3. He knew they rested on the Sabbath. After working six days with his hands, he welcomed a day to worship God and to teach about the Messiah.
      4. He went where no other Christian had gone. There was no congregation there of Believers. He labored single-handed and alone. (Example to all succeeding preachers.)

III. WHAT DID HE PREACH?

A. Jesus, the Messiah. Two main thoughts emphasized.

1. The Jewish Messiah was to be a suffering Messiah. Isaiah (Chp. 53)
2. Jesus of Nazareth was that Messiah. cf. Acts 13:32-43

IV. WHAT WAS THE RESULT? IT FOLLOWS A PATTERN.

A. The result is not always gratifying nor successful.

1. At first, there was success. Acts 13:44
2. Then comes trouble. Acts 13:45 Jews rebelled. 18:6
3. Gentiles rejoiced. Acts 13:48
4. In Corinth, Paul was forced out of the synagogue, but found a place to preach in the house of Titus Justus. 18:7
5. The ruler of the synagogue was converted. 18:8
6. Many Corinthians believed and were baptized. 18:8
7. Here Paul had a year and a half ministry. 18:11

Many are the stories that are told of evangelists, both small and great. Let us learn that even among the Apostles there were times of failure, and only the tenacity given by God could sustain the men engaged in the conflict with God's enemies.

Paul informs us that his preaching was not in grand eloquence and oratory, but in the converting power of the Holy Spirit. His preaching was not in earthly wisdom, but in the hidden wisdom which had not entered into the heart of man until God revealed it. His preaching was not in self-conceit, but in a conscious feebleness and fear and deep anxiety. He did not appeal to the sensational nor the philosophical themes, but he held to one unchangeable theme; Jesus, the Messiah, crucified for lost sinners.

Here we see how God uses the things that the world judges as foolish to put to shame the worldly wise. Those things which the world considers destitute of influence were used to put its powerful influences to shame. Paul put out of existence the things the world thought great and he did it with the things the world considers base. Why did he build the foundation of the church in Corinth on such a foundation? He knew that it was the only foundation that would last, and that it would forever prevent mortal man from boasting in the presence of God, the Almighty.

Let us build the same foundation as Paul laid 1900 years ago; it may be slow, but it is sure. Men may ridicule our progress, but God's smile of approval is still sought by God's men.

"THE CHURCH AT CORINTH"

I Cor. 1:2-3

INTRODUCTION:

The man Paul, who had done the work of an evangelist among them, according to I Cor. 9:2, was a unique combination of humility and authority. At times he was self-depreciation personified and at other times he was very self-assertive. He knew his own unworthiness, and referred to himself as the least of the Apostles. "Not worthy to be called an apostle" in one breath, and yet he defended his Apostleship and does not hesitate in the least to command the churches; even daring to rebuke one of the foremost Apostles of Christ, Peter.

Why was he that type of a man? Because he realized that his office was not due to any previous service of his own, nor that he had appointed himself to it, but rather that he was a chosen vessel of God and Christ, appointed to do a tremendous work among churches in the busiest parts of the world. God had given him a position to which he could not have aspired, himself. He knew God was with him so he feared no man, and willingly faced insurmountable odds. This made him humble, yet confident; he could stand alone and follow a lonely path. Conscious of God's approval and sustained by that consciousness, he could go on against the disapprovals of the whole world.

PROPOSITION: *Note four distinguishing features of the church.*

I. CONSECRATION; "them that are sanctified in Christ Jesus."
   A. The true church's strength is in its consecrated members.
      1. Here sanctified means those who have been set apart or destined for a holy purpose.
      2. Christ used it the same way when He said, "For your sakes I sanctify (set apart) myself."
      3. The church, by its calling, is a body of men and women set apart for God's holy use.
      4. The church is "Called out" to serve God. (One Purpose)
      5. Christians are devoted and set apart to attain perfection in living for Christ. They have a new destiny.

II. SAINTS; "called to be saints."
   A. The word "saints," comes from the root word that means: "made holy."

1. This is an unmistakable characteristic of the church.
2. The essence of the glory of God is his holiness; eternally doing what is BEST, loving and just.
3. It was the churches daily task to exhibit in human life the holiness of God.
4. To think of God doing wrong is blasphemy, and it should be as much so for His children.
5. Christians are treading on dangerous ground when they do anything that is wrong.
6. When Paul found a member in scandalous sin, he said, "put away from among yourselves that wicked person."
7. Communion with others of lesser sins, such as covetous, or an idolater, or a railer, a drunkard or extortioner, was to be cut off. I Cor. 5:11 They were to be a holy people.

III. CATHOLICS; "all that in every place call upon the name of Jesus Christ."
   A. The church is not for one place nor age; but every place.
      1. Christ's church, as set up by the apostles under the guidance of the Holy Spirit, is Universal.
      2. The universality of the church does not depend upon an organization, but upon the Spirit of Christ in each of its members; that is the badge they wear.
      3. Christ's church contains all of Christ's people.
      4. At the same time it contains NONE of the devil's people; they "Can not see the kingdom of God."

IV. UNITED; "Both their Lord and ours."
   A. Christ prayed for this very thing. John chp. 17.
   B. Paul appeals to their ONENESS.
   C. He condemns them for the divisions among them. 1:10
   D. There is one Lord of all the assemblies; loyalty to him, makes ONE people.
   E. By allegiance to him, they are held together and called together. (This must be the VISIBLE church.)
   F. Jesus knew man's peculiar nature and he called for unity that the world might believe.
   G. The trivial things that divided the church there were severely condemned and Christ was pointed out as the focal point of unity.
   H. Outward unity can only come from an INward unity; genuine respect for the Lord and his word.

I. Paul appeals to them to come back to Christ; not to any of their great preachers; for Christ is the source and center of unity.

When he found disunity, Paul did not advocate all of the people in Corinth joining one of the denominations. He said, "Is CHRIST divided?" He associated the church immediately with Christ. No man has the right to make any other church than that which Christ has already established. It is up to all divided humanity who profess belief in Christ to leave all the man-made divisive items and return to a "Thus saith the Lord," and have unity in HIM. He built HIS church and all its members were once united. We can be again! God will hold every man accountable if he does not try to bring Consecration, Holiness, and Unity in the body of Christ, which is His church.

"CHURCH BUILDING BLOCKS"

I Corinthians 1:4

INTRODUCTION:

The church in Corinth was like any other congregation, made up of various types of building material. Some of the members were of the self-righteous and conceited Jews, and some were of the sophisticated Greeks. Some of them were free men, but more than likely the vast majority were bondmen. No doubt there were some of the high ranking society members, but far out numbering them were the men and women of humble stations in life. Corinth represents the most cosmopolitan congregation to which Paul preached or wrote; certainly it was the one possessing the most discord.

PROPOSITION: *What were some of the problems Paul faced and we can expect to face in our Ministries?*

I. HE HAD TO FACE AN ENDLESS WAR OF WORDS. I Cor. 1:17 and 2:13
   A. Because of this sad condition, Paul reminds them that he did not appeal to their system of promoting the kingdom of God.
      1. His work was done by speaking God's wisdom.
         a. He declares his speech was by inspiration. (2:10-13)
      2. He established the church in Corinth by "demonstration of the Spirit and of power." 2:4

II. PAUL HAD TO MEET PERSONAL VANITY AND RIVALRIES IN THE LIVES OF THE MEMBERSHIP. 3:21; 4:6; 7:5-6; II Cor. 10:12; 11:12

A. Paul told them NOT to glory in men, because they were in need of that admonition.

B. This is shown especially in 1:12. It is an age-old affliction of the church membership and will continue to plague the loyal preacher.

C. There were those who made themselves the measuring rod for all others; comparing others with their own attainments. II Cor. 10:12

D. There were those in the church who gloried when they should have been ashamed. II Cor. 11:12 + I Cor. 5:2.

1. They gloried in their shame. Phil. 3:19

E. All these problem children, Paul had to deal with and the faithful preacher can expect no less.

III. THERE WAS A GENERAL LAXITY OF MORALS AND MANNERS.

A. This is reproved in I Cor. 5:11-12 and the manner of dealing with it is plainly stated in verse 13.

1. Paul was not a "Love everybody, hate nobody, middle of the road appeaser." He had God-given standards.

B. There were those in the congregation who were in deliberate rebellion and must be rebuked. I Cor. 6:9ff.

1. The reason for listing these ungodly sins was because they were present in the church membership. Paul knew what would be the result if they were not exposed and halted.

2. He urged them to remember the moral condition in which he had found them. I Cor. 6:11a

3. He reminds them that they had been made holy, sanctified, and justified through Christ. 11b.

This should be the constant work of the evangelist who wants to be a good minister; saving those that hear him, as well as himself. I Tim. 4:16

IV. SOME IN THE CONGREGATION THOUGHT MORE OF THEIR OWN CONVENIENCE THAN THEY DID OF THE WELFARE OF THE CHURCH. I Cor. 10:23-24

A. Selfishness does not die out easily in any heart and it is ever present to defile. The preacher should remember this.

B. Thoughtfulness of others is mandatory in the Christian life. Romans 14:13 "No occasion of falling." We are held accountable whether the brother falls or not.
   1. Paul lived what he preached, relative to this doctrine of "Thinking of the man before we do of ourselves." I Cor. 10:31-11:1
   2. Paul knew that selfishness would kill the church for it advertises the unregenerate heart.

In every corn field there are sickly plants as well as those of luxuriant appearance; supplying a fit emblem of the various characters which compose the true Church of Christ. Some indeed are stunted in their growth by various causes; while others ripen in the full measure of the stature of Christ, having received a larger measure of the spirit of Grace, and engaged a more copious effusion of the Son of Righteousness. Yet all these must be expected to be in the field until harvest. Each has separate uses, as the wise husbandman is careful to keep down the weeds so the crop may grow, so the preacher constantly cultivates the corn, and hoes the weeds.

We are thankful that the errors and mistakes of the members do not become more abundant than the true doctrine of God. Let us strive unto perfection, and let the purpose of God work through us daily, that we may make the church a true Bride of Christ, without spot or wrinkle.

"WHY THE DIVISION?"

I Corinthians 1:10-13

INTRODUCTION:

Beginning with verse ten and through the fourth chapter, Paul is dealing with the quenching of the factious spirit that existed in the Corinthian ecclesiastical circles. He did not cover up the source of his information about them, but told them of whom he had received the information and accusations he was about to make against them. The danger of the selfish factious spirit was so great, that Paul launched immediately into admonishing them to cease arguing and fighting and become one in Spirit and judgment.

Paul does not address his letter to a "Party" in the church, but to ALL the saints in Corinth; the whole church united.

Apparently the parties in the church had not outwardly separated from one another. They still worshipped together although it was common knowledge that they were divided into parties among themselves.

PROPOSITION: *Why were they divided?*

One might answer this question immediately by saying, "they were divided over preachers," and that would be true; however, it would not be the whole truth with application to our status today. I want this sermon to be helpful, so let us look a little deeper.

I. PAUL MENTIONS FIRST THOSE WHO HAD MADE A DIVISION IN THE BODY OF CHRIST BASED ON HIS RELATIONSHIP TO THEM.
   A. All preachers, who have ministered in any place, leave behind them friends and supporters. This is as it should be.
      1. Some owed their personal salvation to Paul.
      2. He had effectively reached them by his methods, and they believed no other man or method was quite as effective.
      3. They lost sight of Christ and His position in the church in their effort to exalt Paul.
      4. They became more Pauline than Paul.
      5. Paul knew they could easily become more Pauline than Christian.
   B. Their indebtedness to Paul for his bringing them the message of salvation was causing them to neglect the Lord he had presented.

II. THE SECOND "PARTY GROUP" PAUL MENTIONS WAS OF APOLLOS.
   A. He was a former preacher of learning and eloquence.
      1. He was the irrigator and cultivator of what Paul had planted.
      2. Some thought they would have died without his ministration, so they felt that they owed him everything.
         a. He had opened to them the relationship of the Gospel as it had bearing on daily living.
         b. He had built a good building upon Paul's foundation; gold, silver and precious stones.
      3. The truth of Paul's statements they accepted, but it was Apollos who gave it sufficient definiteness to cause them to act upon it.

a. They could have reasoned: "We are not opposing the teaching of Paul, we are merely supplementing it."
b. It is good to love former preachers; revere them for their faithfulness to our souls, but it is a heinous sin to cause separations in the church over former preachers.

III. PETER IS NAMED AS THE CENTRAL FIGURE OF THE FACTIOUS MINDED CHURCH MEMBERS IN CORINTH.
A. True, Peter was the Apostle to the circumcision.
1. Peter was known by reputation even though it is possible that he had never been in Corinth.
a. Some people love preachers whom they know only by reputation.
2. Peter would stand in contrast to Paul.
a. He was one of the original group of the Jewish element who were emphasizing the keeping of the Mosaic law.
b. We do not know how disparagingly they had spoken against Paul in Corinth, but in other places they had purposely and openly opposed him.
3. Apparently they accused him, (because of his self denial), of not being equal with Peter.
a. He had no wife, as Peter had.
b. They tried to make his claim to his apostleship insecure.
4. How humiliating it must have been for the high-minded Apostle to have to defend himself against such accusations. (cf. I Cor. 9:1-14)

IV. THE FOURTH PARTY IN THE CHURCH HAD BEEN THE ONLY PARTY IN THE BEGINNING.
A. They had all been of Christ; He is not divided.
B. He was crucified for them.
C. They had been baptized into Him.
D. They wore His name and not the divisive names of men.
E. They had all been of the same mind and judgment before the factions of men came in.
1. This was the very thing for which Paul pleaded.

Basil Holt once said, "Two men had climbed up two opposite branches of a tree. They became more separated the farther they climbed up their respective branches. How could they get together? They were once together, until they separated onto the two branches. They must descend to the trunk if they would ever get together. By returning to their original position, they will return to each other."

This is the only way Christian Unity will ever be achieved. Each split must climb down the branch and back to the trunk, Christ.

"ONLY TWO CHOICES PRESENTED"

I Corinthians 1:18

INTRODUCTION:

Sometimes, I wish there was only one way to go and no possibility of going the wrong way. Perhaps it would be nice if we could go the wrong way or the right way, plus another way just comfortably in the middle; but God has given us just two choices, either right or wrong.

This text, which speaks of them that perish and them that are saved, is not referring to heaven or hell in this particular instance. It is referring to the condition they were in at that present time. They were in the process of coming to a final decision on the religion presented by Paul. Some heard it and perished, others heard it and were saved by accepting its proffered gift.

PROPOSITION: *There are only two choices, with opposite results.*

I. ONE CLASS CHOSE THE WAY OF SAFETY.
   A. They asked "What must we do to be saved?" and then accepted the answer that was given. Acts 2:37-41 + 16:29-34
   B. They wanted to know how to progress.
      1. They asked Jesus to teach them to pray. Luke 11:1
      2. They inquired about holiness of life. Rom. 6:1-2
      3. They were instructed in the way of life. Tit. 2:11-12
      4. They wanted to rise ever higher, with Christ as their standard. I Peter 1:13-16 + Eph. 5:1
   C. They recognized and welcomed the good. "Walked as children of light." Eph. 5:7-12 + 5:15-17
   D. They could see Moral beauty, and Christian duty. Eph. 6:10-20
   E. They have a tender conscience like Paul. Acts 23:1 + Acts 24:16 He could be appealed to.

1. Paul appealed to Timothy to have a good conscience.
   a. This comes from obedience to the will of God. I Tim. 1:5
2. They did not have hardened hearts. Lu. 8:15
   a. They heard the message of the Cross honestly and responded to the Holy Spirit's call.

II. THE OTHER CLASS CHOSE THE WAY OF DANGER.

A. They chose the way of everlasting ruin like the Gadarenes. Luke 8:37
   1. They chose to Believe NOT. John 3:36; Mark 16:16
   2. They chose hardness of heart. Mark 16:14; Ecc. 8:11
   3. Their heart is desperately wicked. Jere. 17:9
   4. They chose to waste their lives. Luke 15:11-16
   5. They chose undoing themselves. Acts 2:13
   6. They chose to go farther and farther from God. The road to hell is down hill. Heb. 3:8-12 + Luke 11:26
   7. They chose to be impenitent. Rom. 2:5-6
   8. They chose to be blind to the heavenly images. Eph. 4:18-19

B. The way of the Cross, to them, is foolishness.

Surely we may ruin ourselves forever; there is no doubt or limitation there. Right now you may be just beginning to tread that dreadful pathway. On the other hand, we may save ourselves by heeding the message of the Cross and obeying the Lord of our Salvation. We are to walk dutifully with God, trust Him, and come back to Him whenever we have offended Him, however deeply. He is abundantly able to pardon unto the uttermost. In this way He will save you; save you daily. The God who is able to save us and cleanse us from a life of sin, is able to wash us and keep us daily if we will yield to the way of the Cross and walk in the wisdom of God.

We are all called, however our wisdom is seen in the manner in which we respond. In the early twenties of this century an old prospector took his gun to go into the hills to get his "meat" for the winter. He told his friend that he would be back "Someday." His friend thought nothing about the old man's manner of speech until he did not show up for two weeks. Usually he was out and back within a week's time. Thinking possibly the old man had slipped and fallen, he went out in search for him. He shot his gun ever so many times and yelled, "Frank!" There was no response.

After three days of searching he called into town to get assistance in the search. They looked for several days. Off and on all winter he would take a day to go out and look, but no Frank was to be found.

Early the next summer two men were tramping through the woods, not more than half a mile from the old man's camp, when they stumbled upon something covered partially by leaves. Looking closer they found a shoe and then the partially decomposed body of a man in rugged mountain clothes. They searched, and under the boney and wild animal gnawed body, they found a leather bill fold. Inside of it was the identification card of the old miner, but what amazed them more was a note scribbled in heavy pencil, "I heard you call, but I would not come."

A warm fire, food, and a comfortable cabin were calling to him, but he would not come; that is a form of suicide. Friends, everlasting life in the most beautiful place man can ever imagine calls every time the Gospel of the Cross is preached. You can choose to perish and separate yourself from God forever, or you can be wise and be saved from all your sin, by "the power of God."

"FOOLISHNESS OF PREACHING"

I Corinthians 1:21

INTRODUCTION:

The "preaching" referred to here is not merely the public proclamation by voice; it is not Euangelizo, "to declare good news." The word is not Kerusso which signifies "a herald." Paul chooses carefully the words used by Inspiration and skips over Parrhesiazomai too which means, "to speak boldly." He uses Kerugma here, which denotes "the message preached," or the "substance of what is preached," in contrast to the act of preaching.

Some preachers, I suppose, think that the more foolish the preaching the more power in it, judging from the amount of levity and downright foolishness that pours from the "luke-warm fountain" on Sunday morning. But here be it noted that it pleased God to use what the world calls a foolish message, ("Christ crucified") to save them that believe. It is not mere discourse, nor oratory that saves men; it is THE SUBSTANCE OF THE MESSAGE FROM HEAVEN that brings salvation to the believer.

PROPOSITION: *Note three definite parts to this message and the results. (As evidenced in this text.)*

I. WHAT WAS THE CONTENT OF THE MESSAGE?

A. It was a positive and definite message; just ONE.

1. It rested on a solid, evident foundation.
   - a. It was based on the history of a "God led" people and the promises made to them. Gen. 12:1-4
   - b. It was the outcome of centuries of Prophecies leading to its culmination. Isa. chap. 53.
   - c. It was the plan laid from the beginning. Rev. 13:8
   - d. It was planted in broad daylight on the earth, in light of history, raising its head toward heaven. Acts 26:26
2. It unveiled to the believer the inner being of God. John 3:16 Strange doctrine then, and now.
3. It displayed the manner in which God revealed Himself. Phil. 2:6-8
4. It made known to man the bridge God had constructed to cover the abyss that sin had created between man and his God.
5. It announced man's forgiveness through the fountain that cleanses and gives hope of eternal pardon, plus the grace of God that comes to dwell in us daily, giving victory. Acts 5:32 + Gal. 5:22-23

II. WHAT WAS THE OBJECT OF THE MESSAGE THE WORLD CONSIDERED FOOLISH?

A. It was to "Save them that believe." Mark 16:15-16

1. Believing was based upon evidence. Rom. 10:17
2. Peter used this same method on Pentecost. Acts 2:40 "With many other words did he testify."

B. Salvation here is to save the individual human soul from ruin caused by past sins.

1. Sin, begun here, if continued to the grave is irretrievable.

C. Christ was set forth by Paul as "Evidently crucified" to save sinners from eternal death.

1. Jesus believed that men were headed for eternal hell if they were not saved. Matt. 25:46

D. Christ, by His death, become the world's all sufficient Saviour. "He is able also to save them to the uttermost that come unto God by him. . ." Heb. 7:25

III. WHO WERE TO RECEIVE THIS SALVATION? "THEM THAT BELIEVE."

A. The group to be saved represents a limited class of people: Believers. John 3:16; 3:36; Acts 4:4; 8:12; Rom. 1:16

B. Believing is the first step in salvation, all else is based upon it.

1. Repentance, confession and baptism are worthless unless they stem from a Believing heart. How true it is, "He that believeth NOT, shall be damned."

C. Belief is a movement of our whole soul going forth to meet God's appointed truth.

1. It is thought.
2. It is trust.
3. It is affection.
4. It is complete surrender to the unseen Christ.

It is faith in the efficacy of the crucified Christ that brings to our souls salvation. Every other step in our salvation is based upon that one element... FAITH, BELIEVING! Not faith alone, but faith foundational; Faith that produces faithfulness.

Faith is seen in the way people react to the message of the cross. On Pentecost, "Those that received his word were baptized." Why were they baptized? Because they believed the word Peter had preached, offering salvation from sins and the gift of the Holy Spirit to those who believed in the Crucified and Resurrected Christ. When they BELIEVED the message they asked, "What shall we do?" Because they believed, they asked. When they were told to be baptized for the remission of their sins, because of their faith, they obeyed and the Christ in whom they believed took away their sins by His propitiatory sacrifice.

"It pleased God by the foolishness of preaching to save them that believed."

"WISDOM OF WORDS Vs. THE CROSS OF CHRIST"

I Corinthians 1:17-24

INTRODUCTION:

Here Paul leaves the immediate subject he had been discussing, <u>divisions among them</u>, and reverts to the cause of their existence in the first place. It was his preaching that gave them birth as a congregation. He had not appealed to some sort of a new philosophy presented in the fine rhetoric and flamboyant extravaganza of high sounding euphony in which the Greeks reveled. He reminds them that this preaching was his purpose among them. They had been baptized into Christ as a result of his preaching the "Cross of Christ," and not some "Wisdom of the world."

PROPOSITION: *Notice the theme preached, how it was preached, and the results.*

I. THE THEME OF PAUL'S PREACHING...THE CROSS OF CHRIST
   A. It was "The Word of the Cross" or Christ crucified according to I Cor. 1:18, 1:23 and 2:2.
   B. If there was ever an excuse to "Doctor up" the simple message, it would have been in Corinth and Athens; but Paul "stuck to his guns," so to speak, and preached the simple gospel message.
   C. Philosophers and world teachers laid stress upon "Wisdom of words," but Paul preached Christ and Him crucified. 2:2
      1. Paul did not evade the "Blood." He would not have voted to take the blood out of the song book.
      2. Paul "Gloried in the Cross," because that was the one pre-eminent thing that distinguished his message from high sounding moral philosophies.
      3. Phil. 2:8 was the foundation of his message. This is the "Pass word" that gains entrance into salvation, for without the shedding of blood there is no remission.
      4. Paul did not try to match wits nor wisdom with Socrates, Epictetus nor Plato; he appealed to ALL mankind. Christ was presented as the Redeemer of ALL people everywhere by His death on the Cross.
   D. The message of the cross answered the age old question of how a man can be right before God, after he has sinned.
      1. It was salvation by a propitiatory sacrifice. Rom. 3:25-26
      2. Christ, God's own Son, suffering for the many sinners. Eph. 1:7, I John 1:7; Rom. 5:9-10; Heb. 9:22

II. HOW WAS THIS MESSAGE CARRIED?
   A. By pure evangelical preaching of the Good News.
      1. Paul believed what he taught. Rom. 10:9-17
      2. He obeyed the last command of Jesus. Mark 16:15-16
      3. He set an example for all generations to follow; his great life of Missionary activity.

a. He was not speculating about the death of a Martyr. Paul's sermons appealed to the heart and conscience.
b. He did not hide the cross behind a barrage of highly ethical and technical philosophical terms.
c. He did not decorate his message until the heart and the cross were covered up in "Roses."
d. Paul preached Good News as a herald of the Lord Jesus, and in strict obedience to His command.

III. HOW WAS THIS MESSAGE RECEIVED BY THOSE WHO HEARD?
A. First to those who would not believe.
1. Their attitude, caused by education, environment, and former teaching, affected the minds of the hearers.
2. The Jews with their background, asked for signs. Vs. 22
a. They treated Jesus the same way. Matt. 12:38
b. Jesus rebuked them for this request. Matt. 12:39
c. Where it was necessary, Jesus did work miracles. Mk 2:3-12 John 5:5-9
d. There were enough miracles that Nicodemus was convinced that Jesus was a "Man from God." John 3:1-3
3. The second group of Unbelievers were the Greeks. They sought after wisdom; wisdom that was of man's concoction. (Philosophies)
a. A crucified leader could not be a victorious leader in their realm of thinking; to them it was foolishness. Vs. 23
b. From a purely philosophical standpoint, it was ridiculous that a defeated man could give victory. He should have been successful to appeal to them.
c. Jesus had explained to the Greeks in John 12:21-25 that He must die to bring forth Life; this they did not believe.
d. A crucified Redeemer was sheer folly to their enlightened minds. (We have some of these in pulpits today)
e. Blood doctrine to them is very distasteful and they vote it out of the curriculum in their Seminaries.
f. Paul reminded them that the world in its wisdom knew not God; they had failed utterly to find Him in their search for wisdom!

B. Thank God there were those who believed. Vs. 24 (The Called) Termed as being saved in vs. 18; Believers vs. 21
   1. They heeded the call of the Gospel message and came out of whatever background hindered them.
   2. They believed in this Atoning Saviour who could make all men JUST before God. In the heart of the Believer the power of God is working unto Salvation.
      a. Out of Faith grows repentance, an honest confession of source of our faith, and obedience to him in Baptism, for the remission of our sins.
   3. His Holy Spirit makes them New Creatures in Christ Jesus. They became a witness to the power of the message of the Cross.
      a. From then on they live as one brought from darkness to light, from damnation to salvation and from infidelity to fidelity.

This message of the Cross began in Jerusalem 2,000 years ago and has gone to the uttermost parts of the world, working as effectively today as it did then. It is God's only method for the salvation of wayward men who have missed the mark. Eph. 2:8-9

A Missionary once gave this report concerning the island where he ministered. "Fifteen years ago they lived in brush as brutes, (Anarchy) war and bloodshed prevailed, they were strangers to prayer and praise, they were naked and without a moral standard of life; but now they have neat plastered cottages, they have law, order and peace, they are clothed and in their right minds having prayer around the family altar. They have a written language in which to read the message of the Cross. Over four hundred men and women have been saved from lives of sin. The influence of the gospel has permeated every strain of life on this island."

It can do as much for you, no matter whether you are rich or poor, educated or ignorant, deep in sin or just skating on the thin ice of hell's crust.

The wisdom of God, which men call foolishness, has been proven to be wiser than the greatest wisdom of men. Oh friend, accept Him now as your "Lamb" sent forth from God to die in your stead.

"THE CONSTITUENCY OF THE LORD'S CHURCH"

I Corinthians 1:26-29

INTRODUCTION:

This gives us an insight into the actual membership of the church in Corinth. It was certainly composed of the ignoble. It is very evident that they did not attain membership in the mystical "Body of Christ" by human wisdom, nor by the power they inherentaly possessed, nor by anything that was generally accepted as the key to entrance into the occult societies of the day. They did not retain their position as saved men and women by being able to recite Homer, Aristotle or even Scripture. Memory, much as it was honored among the Greeks, was not the admission token.

PROPOSITION: *Of what did the membership consist?*

Negatively stated:

I. THEY WERE NOT ADMITTED MEMBERSHIP IN HIS CHURCH BY THEIR OWN WISDOM. 1:26 "Not many wise after the flesh are called."
   A. If "human wisdom" had been the power to open the Gates of Christ's kingdom, I am sure there would be a thinning of the ranks! It is just as true today.
   B. Being "wise in our own minds" is not the passport into the presence of God. Jesus did not call the Philosophers in the temple area to be His apostles; but He called humble men of the sea.
   C. Men, by their wisdom, had never been able to find God. 1:21
      1. Witness the great assembly of "wisemen" who led their devotees deeper and deeper into the morass of intertwining and endless speculations that had no certainty of answer.
   D. Even in the Old Testament God did not choose Bablylon, Assyria, Persia or Greece as the nation through which He would work.
   E. Because of their nobility of character, men were not necessarily commended to God.
   F. It is GOD who calls men; usually the less of the worldly wisdom they possess, the more readily they listen to Him. He chose the foolish to confound the wise. 1:27

II. THEY WERE NOT ADMITTED CHURCH MEMBERSHIP BECAUSE OF THEIR PROMINENT POSITIONS IN THE WORLD. "Not many mighty are called."

A. The appeal was not to Caesar, Pilate, or Herod.

B. Paul was humbled before God could use him. Acts 9:3-16

1. His confession in later years was... I Tim. 1:12-16

C. The sermon seems to be of small effect in Athens. Acts 17:18-33

D. Those doctors of philosophy, who in later centuries openly accepted Christ, usually brought with them rank heresies.

1. Witness Tertullian and Augustine.
   Positions in politics, business or state-craft do not make any impression upon God in calling men.

III. THEY WERE NOT CALLED BECAUSE THEY WERE OF THE NOBILITY. "Not many noble are called."

A. Paul did not go to the city council in Philippi but to the riverside where lowly women met to pray. Acts 16:13

B. They had a better hearing in the jail among prisoners than they had among the aristocracy. Acts 16:19-23

C. It had been the "Ruling class" of despicable ecclesiastical "Nobility" that had caused Jesus the most trouble. Matt. 23:13-35 plus Matt. 27:1-2; 11-12; 20

D. In order to be used of God a man must be big enough to become small enough to be pliable in God's hands. Witness Moses.

E. Paul admonished the Roman Christians in this. Romans 12:16 plus Vs. 3

1. Pride of birth or station is an almost insurmountable barrier to entrance into Christ's church.

Positively stated:

I. GOD HAS CHOSEN THE FOOLISH THINGS TO PUT TO SHAME THE WISE. Vs. 27

A. What philosopher ever conjured up a plan of redemption where the Gods willingly offered up a Son of Deity in order to save, justify and reconcile lost men and women? They considered that a "Foolish" doctrine, but notice it has worked.

II. GOD HAS CHOSEN THE WEAK THINGS OF THE WORLD TO CONFOUND THE THINGS OF THE MIGHTY. Vs. 27 (Weak people composed it)

A. Who but Jesus would choose "ignorant and unlearned" men

to commence and carry out the gospel of salvation to the whole world? Acts 4:13 These men, filled with the Holy Spirit, "turned the world upside down."--Acts 17:6

B. The appeal of these "Weak" men to the common citizenry of the Roman empire shook it to its foundations and caused wave after wave of persecutions from the Emperor this succeeded only in making immortal martyrs.

III. GOD CHOSE THE THINGS THAT "ARE NOT." Vs. 28.

A. God's program was not built upon a showy Temple adherence, but upon a verbal message.
B. It demanded FAITH, something that can not be seen, had no form or visible appearance. Heb. 11:6
C. It brought REPENTANCE, another invisible potent part of Christianity. Upon these two "are nots," "invisibles," the whole structure and superstructure of the Church of Christ is built.
D. No flesh could glory in the presence of God because of the despised things out of which His kingdom was built. Vs. 29
E. The things that "Were not" have outlasted the temporal and material things the Romans considered so enduring. Christ's kingdom, His church, lives today and the Gates of Hades shall never prevail against it!

The church still appeals to that which the Romans despised, the death of Christ by crucifixion, for the atoning of the sins of the world.

When the Moravians opened a mission in Greenland, they found the natives so ignorant that they decided to educate them first before preaching Christ to them. They failed utterly and decided to go home. One of them decided to read to the natives from his translation of the Bible before leaving. He had translated the account of the crucifixion of Christ and he read it to the assembled natives. Upon finishing the account the chief asked, "Is that story true?" They assured him it was. Then he asked, "Why did you not tell us that at first? You must not leave us now. We will listen to the words of the Man who suffered for us." So the foolishness and weakness of the Cross, won where education failed.

"WHAT DOES THIS CALLING GIVE THE CHRISTIAN?"

I Corinthians 1:30

INTRODUCTION:

In the field of philosophy, men glory in their attainments, intellectually. They glory in their tasseled caps in the fourth position, their gowns of various hue and the letters after their names; but it is NOT so "In Christ." What we enjoy from the Lord is a GIFT that we did not earn, "That no flesh should glory before God." Vs. 29 "He that glorieth, let him glory in the Lord." Vs. 31. We have, in Christ, the greatest gifts possible for man to attain, freely given us in the Beloved. The more we understand the preciousness of these gifts, the more precious is our Salvation.

PROPOSITION: *What has Christ been made unto us, as His children?*

I. HE IS THE WISDOM FROM GOD.
   A. In comparison with man's wisdom, it is incomparable. Vs. 2
      1. His wisdom is perfect. Job 36:4-5 + 37:16
      2. His wisdom is Unsearchable. Isa. 40:28; Rom. 11:33
      3. His wisdom is beyond human comprehension. Psa. 139:1-6
      4. His wisdom is incomparable. Isa. 44:6-7; Jere. 10:7
   B. Its source is beyond man's reach.
      1. It is in the Gospel. I Cor. 2:6-9
      2. It is so simple, wise men stumble over it; yet children who desire His truth, find it readily. Matt. 11:25-26
      3. This is the new law of life for those in Christ, even as the old law led Israel. Ezra 7:25

In Christ Jesus we have a wisdom above all that is known to man, and from a source that is attainable to all those desiring it.

II. HE IS OUR RIGHTEOUSNESS.
   A. "All have sinned, and fall short of the glory of God." Rom. 3:23
      1. We needed God's righteousness, because none by nature have it. Job. 15:14; Rom. 3:10-18
      2. God's righteousness, found in Christ, is sufficient. 2 Cor. 5:21; It is imputed to us. Rom. 4:11-22
      3. We should follow after it. Isa. 51:1
      4. We should hunger and thirst after it. Matt. 5:6

5. We should put no trust in our own. Phil. 3:6-8
   What a comfort it is to KNOW we are right in God's sight.

III. HE IS OUR SANCTIFICATION. Heb. 2:11-12
   A. We have holiness of life in no other way than by Christ.
      1. Our holiness is through His atonement. Heb. 10:10; 13:12
      2. Our remaining holy, is through His blood. I John 1:7-10
      3. The church is made glorious through this holiness. Eph. 5:26-27

CONCLUSION:

We are cleansed from all our past sins by Christ, and kept clean by His blood as represented in the Lord's supper.

IV. HE IS OUR REDEMPTION. Matt. 20:28
   A. We have no other means of gaining purity except by being bought back.
      1. Christ was sent to effect our redemption. Gal. 4:4-5
      2. It is His blood that made way for our Redemption. Heb. 9:12 and Rev. 5:9
         a. We are redeemed from the curse of the Law. Gal. 3:13
         b. We are redeemed from the power of sin. Rom. 6:18-22
         c. We are redeemed from this present evil world. Gal. 1:4
   B. This procured for us the forgiveness of all our past sins. Eph. 1:7

CONCLUSION:

I have just returned from visiting a man in prison whom I had never met. His former girl friend had called me and asked if I would go to see him. He has been a hard working man but one who has left Christ out of his life and has avoided the church. Now he is in jail charged with drunk driving, receiving and transporting stolen goods and his bail is set at $5,000.00. Just think what a change it would have made in his life if he had used some of the wisdom of God, lived according to God's righteousness, let the blood of Christ sanctify him, and lived as though he had been redeemed and appreciated it.

He once attended church, but now evil companionships have corrupted the good morals that he once had. He is facing another trial after he serves this ninety-day sentence and that may be a felony charge. Possibly, he is headed for the state Penitentiary.

We can all see this man's predicament readily, but every person who has not been saved from his past sins by Christ, the Redeemer, is charged by God with a "felony," and headed for a court where there is no polluting the jury nor "buying off" the judge. The sinners sentence is already pronounced by the unchanging God; "The wages of sin is death," The jail is eternal hell.

My prayer is that you will come to Christ and find in Him your wisdom, righteousness, holiness and God's redemption.

"WHY PREACH CHRIST AND HIM CRUCIFIED?"

I Corinthians 2:1-2

INTRODUCTION:

There was much that Paul could have preached about Jesus that would have commended Him to both the Jew and the Greek. Why then did he introduce the subject that was a stumbling block to the Jews and foolishness to the Greeks...the crucifixion of Christ. Paul could have told the Jews that Jesus was one of their own countrymen. He could have dwelt long on Christ's wonderful miraculous power or His sermon on the mount, with all its beauty or on the fact that He should have been accepted by them because He was an honor to their race. Surely He was a "Hebrew of the Hebrews;" he was honoring the Law of Moses and told His listeners that He had not come to destroy the law but to fulfill it. He urged His audience to search the Scriptures; He referred to them often in His teachings. He could have told them how He preached on the Sabbath day in the synagogue, but he did not!

He could have spoken to the Greeks and Gentiles about how loyally Jesus had submitted to their governments, and all of this would have been pure truth, why then did he dwell upon the awful doctrine of the Crucifixion?

PROPOSITION: *Why preach Christ and Him crucified?*

I. PAUL WAS CONVINCED THAT THERE WAS SOMETHING SPECIAL AND EXTRAORDINARY IN THE DEATH OF CHRIST.
   A. The prophets had spoken much of His death for our remission. Isa. 53:4-8 + 10-12; Daniel 9:24-26; Zech. 13:1-7
      1. This was an appeal to the Jewish mind; He fulfilled prophecy.
   B. Jesus spoke much of His coming death.
      1. He said He was "to give his life a ransom for many." Mark 10:45
      2. He was announced as "The lamb of God, that taketh away the sin of the world!" John 1:29
      3. He prophesied that He must be lifted up even as Moses lifted up the serpent. John 3:14
      4. He said that "the good shepherd layeth down his life for the sheep." John 10:11-14; John 11:50-52
   C. Paul knew that justification must come through the atoning death of Jesus on the cross. Rom. 3:24-25; 5:6-11
      1. Our overcoming death is through the death of Christ. Rom. 6:3-10
      2. Paul knew it was for both Jew and Gentile. Gal. 4:4-6 + Eph. 1:6-7
      3. Paul knew our redemption, peace, forgiveness and reconciliation are in the blood of Christ. Col. 1:14+ 20-22
   D. Paul believed that something more important took place in the death of Christ than had taken place in all of his illustrous life upon the earth.
      1. His death was to bring LIFE to all mankind who would believe and obey Him. Mark 16:15-16
         a. We can only understand Paul's preaching the crucifixion of Christ on this one ground.
         b. Its importance accounts for the prominence he gave it.

II. NOTICE WHAT WOULD HAVE HAPPENED IF HE HAD NOT PREACHED THE CRUCIFIED CHRIST.
   A. If Paul had not made the Crucified Christ the great theme of his ministry, we would never have heard of Christianity.
      1. They might have preached about Christ's noble example until they were "blue in the face," but to no avail.
      2. They might have made reference to His beauty of character, matching him with the excellent character of psychologist's invention, and He would have died as they have.
      3. If there had been no Cross, then we would have known no Christ.

Their preaching would have been forgotten, but Christ crucified is an eternal truth that never can come amiss. We today can never emphasize enough that in spite of the Corinthians' sinfulness and alienation, God (the God Paul preached) still loved them. The cross of Christ was the greatest way in which this love could be expressed. The Son of God suffered humiliation for the sons of men. This was the greatest demonstration of Divine love for man that God had shown. This, irresistibly proves, that God so loved them as to do everything to save them except to dishonor Himself. No wonder Paul said, "I am determined to know nothing among you save Christ and Him crucified."

Recently a great iron manufacturer imported a giant magnetic crane. They found that when one of the magnets passed over the ground it recovered thousands of pounds of iron that had laid buried for years. Huge pieces of iron fairly leapt through their earthen mantle to meet the mighty magnetic force and many mysterious parts that had been reported "missing" were accounted for.

Christ's death on the cross is much like that. When it is preached and the Holy Spirit works with the message, "Steeled hearts" are pulled to the Saviour on the cross like a mighty magnet, even though they have been buried in sins for years. Jesus says, "And I, if I be lifted up (crucified) will draw all men unto me." He is drawing you right now, my friend, won't you let Him be your Saviour by His death, and won't you do it now?

"A TREMBLING AND FEARFUL PREACHER"

I Corinthians 2:1-3

INTRODUCTION:

Let us analyze Paul's condition. Fresh in his memory were the events that transpired in Athens. It had been practically a failure. They had referred to him as a "babbler" and had treated him with cold disdain. Paul knew that some things hurt worse than the stripes put on one's back by the "Cat of nine tails." He had tried with all his might and had miserably failed.

From there he came to Corinth, a city of much the same social and intellectual level as Athens. Philosophers ranged the streets and market places. He was in a quandry; how would his message be received here?

PROPOSITION: *Why was Paul discouraged and weak?*

I. HIS LABORIOUS LIFE OF SIX DAYS LABOR AND PREACHING ON THE SEVENTH WAS WEARING.
   A. Either one was enough for most strong men. Tent making was difficult.
   B. Many men break under the strain of a ministry less demanding than the one Paul carried on all his later life. Acts 20:18-27; 20:31-38.

II. HE FACED POVERTY OFTEN AND PROBABLY WAS UNDERNOURISHED. Gal. 4:13-14
   A. Wages in that part of the world were low. They always have been and still are.
   B. He was depending upon help from those whom he had served. Philippians 4:10-18

III. HE WAS PROBABLY WEAKENED FROM HIS TRIALS.
   A. Tradition tells us Paul was not too robust at best.
   B. "I was with you in weakness, and in fear, and in much trembling" aptly describes his condition in his own words. 2:3
   C. Anyone can serve God when there are no trials, and his health is in the "Pink"; but it takes a dedicated man of God to serve God when it is difficult. Col. 2:25-30

IV. BITTER AND PERNICIOUS OPPOSITION, CONTINUOUSLY.
   A. The Jews filled with National historical pride, prejudices and passions, always opposed him. Acts 13:50; 23:27; 26:21; 20:3
      1. Paul knew what to expect; he had done the same things. Acts 26:9-11. He recalled his actions.
   B. The Gentiles opposed him, often led by Jews. Acts 14:11-19 I Cor. 16:8

V. DREAD OF PERSONAL VIOLENCE.
   A. Paul was not a physical coward, but if one has any sense he does not want to suffer or be killed.
      1. Even Jesus prayed for the cup to pass away, if it were possible. Matt. 26:39
   B. Only fools have no fear of physical harm. (Or inexperienced)
      1. Any soldier who has gone into battle knows there is fear, dread and quavering inside. Heros act, knowing the danger and fear.

VI. CHURCH PROBLEMS.

A. Judaism was bidding for the Galatian church to unite with it on Judaisers misinformation. Gal. 1:6-10; 2:11-13

B. The Saints at Thessalonica were doubting the Lord's return. I Thess. 4:13-18

VII. THE UNCONSECRATED WEALTH OF THE CITY AND MORAL DECAY.

A. Business flourished, wealth was increased doubly; but men and morals degenerated on every hand. "In Corinth the trouble was not dogma, but deviltry; not dialectics, but degradation; not prophecy; but prostitution; not differences of opinion but chasms in conduct."

VIII. THE LOSS OF SLEEP AND REST.

A. When the long day was done there was little time to rest, and anxiety for all the churches drove sleep from him.

B. Insomnia, or just loss of sleep drives strength away and shatters nerves. We must either sleep or die, or possible land in an institution for the mentally ill.

C. Paul sums it up "by reason of the distress that is upon us." He was facing problems.

God came to his rescue; He always does. He appeared to Moses in the burning bush, to Joshua over against Jericho, and to Elijah in the mouth of the cave. He came to Paul when he was dejected in his heart. God appeared to him in a vision. II Cor. 12:1-6. This is one of the three great visions God gave Paul to strengthen him for great tasks and emergencies. Paul learned, and we can learn too, to keep a stout heart. Remember we are never whipped until we are whipped INside. We are to keep on preaching, even as he did while staying there for a year and a half longer. Acts 18:11 We are immortal until our work is done. There are many people in the city where we preach, and God is depending on us to get the message to them.

History tells us that Paul was victorious, and the same God lives today, upon whom we depend.

"THE WEAK PREACHER'S SOURCE OF STRENGTH"

I Corinthians 2:1-5

INTRODUCTION:

Appearances are deceiving. A man may appear to be very strong. He may be very aggressive in his own power, satisfied with his life, centered in self. He may appear to have vigor of body and mind and completely self reliant. He may be a self contained individual with habits of life developed to give sound judgment and wisdom in all of his activities; but if all he has is himself, in time he will be proven merely human and weak. All it takes is TIME to bring the proud man down in humiliating defeat. Jos. 4:6

On the other hand God has given us the privilege of being agents of His, with His Spirit dwelling within us and giving victory when we are facing defeat in our own strength. His power takes the place of our human frailties and weaknesses, giving Spiritual power to meet the spiritual problems that assail us daily. As agents of the Holy Spirit we do not become proud in ourselves, but we give Him the glory and share in the victories of life.

PROPOSITION: *"How this power is seen in Paul's life!"*

I. PAUL'S UNIMPRESSIVE APPEARANCE.
   A. Tradition has passed on to us that Paul was a small man in stature and we know from the scriptures that he was often ill. Gal. 4:13-14 Possibly he had sore eyes, unsightly.
      1. He tells us often that his speech was not that of a polished rhetorician. Vs. 4-5; II Cor. 11:6
      2. His enemies tried to take advantage of this appearance. I Cor. 9:1-6; II Cor. 13:1-10
      3. The centuries that have past into oblivion have been replete with the names of Saints of God who have been physically handicapped. The preachers I know who are doing things today, practically everyone of them has a handicap of some kind; eyesight, speech, lungs or general physical health.

II. PAUL RECOGNIZED THAT HE WAS FRAIL, BUT GOD IS STRONG.
   A. He depended upon God's power. II Cor. 10:1-2; 10:10; II Cor. 11:21; II Cor. 13:3-4; Philippians 4:13
   B. With this weak body he was enabled of God to suffer stoning and then get up from the "City dump" and go to Derbe to preach his sustaining Christ. Acts 14:8-20
   C. Every preacher must constantly fight his own weaknesses and his feelings of unworthiness to preach the eternal gospel of Christ. Only God's power within enables the preacher to carry on.

III. GOD'S POWER IS SEEN IN THE RESULTS OF PAUL'S MINISTRY.

A. The miracles wrought by him, as witnessed by his congregation, testified to the power that "worketh in me." I Cor. 2:4-5; I Cor. 4:20-21; Rom. 15:18-19

B. The many congregations he established in his short life time, (and that in the very heart of heathenism) witness God's power in him. (All three missionary journeys.)

C. His ability to live through stoning, riots, shipwreck and other troubles testifies to a power beyond his own. II Cor. 11:23-33.

D. The writings of the fourteen New Testament epistles bear witness to Paul's inward power; their preservation only accountable to God's providence. His ability to teach men through the intervening centuries, bears witness that God worked in him.

IV. PAUL GAVE GOD THE GLORY AND FORGED ON IN HIS STRENGTH.

A. Often times people would account for him only by his physical appearance and his human abilities, but Paul knew he was God's man.

   1. This began in Acts 9:20-29 and did not stop until his black curly head rolled away from the guillotine in Rome.
   2. He was God-impowered to overcome his weaknesses.

B. We can attain some of this power through watchfulness, self-denial, fasting and mastery of our human desires.

This example that Paul has given us can be emulated by every follower of Christ, preachers included, for they should lead the way.

In driving piles, a machine is used by which a huge weight is lifted up and then made to fall upon the head of the pile. Of course the higher the weight is lifted the more powerful is the blow when it descends. Now, if we would tell upon our age and come down upon those around us with ponderous blows, we must see to it that we are lifted as near to God as possible.

All of our power depends upon the elevation of our spirits to the source of power, our God. Prayer, meditation, and communion, are like windlasses to wind us aloft. It is not lost time spent in these sacred exercises, for we are thus accumulating force, so that when we come down to our actual labor for God, we shall descend with an energy unknown to those to whom communion is unknown.

Oh, my friend, if you would have the power that moved and blest the Apostle Paul, let Jesus come into your heart and reign there.

"THE QUALITY OF PAUL'S WISDOM"

I Corinthians 2:6-10

INTRODUCTION:

While Paul definitely refused to go along with the "Wisdom of men," he just as definitely declared himself to be a dispenser of "True wisdom." The great principles he preached are basic to genuine wisdom. The plan of redemption that God gave is the most sublime philosophy ever divulged to man. It is so constructed that it is "milk for babes," and at the same time it is "strong meat" for the advanced in learning. Paul proved himself an adept teacher by adapting his teachings to the level of his listeners.

PROPOSITION: *A consideration of Paul's wisdom.*

I. NOTE THE PECULIAR MARKINGS OR QUALITIES OF THIS WISDOM.
   A. It is "not of this world." Vs. 6.
      1. It did not spring from the human element alone.
      2. The great politicians, diplomats, Emperors or Princes could not have invented it; what they promote soon dies.
      3. Paul's God-given wisdom copied nothing from them; his lives through the centuries, while their philosophy dies with them.
   B. This WISDOM came from Jehovah God.
      1. It could only have been the product of a Divine thought.
      2. Every phase of it, from beginning to fruition, speaks of Him.
      3. Its characteristics are those of Deity.
         a. Paul described it as a "Mystery." cf. 4:1 + Eph. 1:9
         b. Only with God's power in us can we understand it.
         c. The silence that had surrounded it was now broken; in the open it becomes blessedly plain. cf. Isa. 35:8
         d. The plan for the salvation of sinful man was premeditated; the way was prepared for his return in the mind

of God before the foundation of the world. cf. I Peter 1:20 This was for our glory.

4. But mystery of mysteries, when the wisdom of Divine origin did come, men who were "wise in their own conceits" did not recognize it for what it was, and crucified the one who had revealed it.

II. FROM WHENCE IS OUR SPIRITUAL WISDOM DERIVED?

A. Paul quoted from the well known prophet Isaiah to prove that it was of Divine origin. Vs. 9-Isa. 64:4

1. This verse is not a description nor reference to heaven. It refers to God's plan for our salvation, pardon, peace, and the gift of eternal life as given in Christ. The world did not know about these and of themselves they could not learn. (It had never entered into the mind of man)
2. All through the Old Testament period this plan was in the process of preparation; gradually it was being unfolded.
3. In the fulness of time God sent forth the final revelation of this wisdom, it is for all who love Him. They could see, hear and feel what the wisest men, in their own foolishness, could never know.

III. HOW IS THIS SPIRITUAL WISDOM ATTAINED?

A. It is not gained through natural faculties. Vss. 6-8

1. It comes not by sight, hearing, nor by their own astuteness in the realm of philosophy.
2. Man has done great things in the material realm, but, in spiritual wisdom without God's revelation he has never advanced beyond kindergarten.

B. The Spirit of God reveals this mystery to us. Vs. 10-John 16:13

1. God gave His Spirit to His chosen men so they could know what was in the mind of God, for man's salvation. Vs. 11
2. Then the spirit of man, enlightend by the Spirit of God, in turn enlightens other poor wandering men. This is God's method of proceedure. Matt. 28:18-20
   a. How it works. Acts 16:14; Gal. 1:15-16

Man's wisdom is seen by what he does with the wisdom of God when it is presented to him in an understandable way. When a man realizes that this message of salvation is the product of the wisdom of God--planned for thousands of years, actually originating in the dim dawn of eternity--then man's wisdom is seen in his response.

Oh! friends, when we realize that God created us so wonderfully, that He revealed Himself to us in such a way that we should love Him, and that our eternal welfare depends upon our turning to our Creator; then let us come to Him and receive His blessing of forgiveness and eternal life, as revealed in this mystery of heavenly wisdom--the atonement by His son.

Can you see Jesus standing in your place and bearing the wrath of God for you, and not melt inside? Can you see yourself bound like Isaac upon the Altar of God's justice and as the knife is raised for the death blow, Christ comes like the ram at Isaac's sacrificial scene to be offered in your stead, and not be moved? Can you see the fearful tempest of your past sins about to overwhelm you by the anger of God, and then Jesus offers Himself to be thrown in the sea in your stead, and not turn to Him in gratitude? Let your heart dwell on this Mystery of God's Wisdom. Can you see Christ as He was taken from the cross, drenched in His own blood; and as you look, say to yourself, "those wounds were for me"--"that is how much He loves me." Then know that from His wounds comes the balm of healing for the wounds that sin has placed on us.

This wisdom of God has been reaching, changing and bringing peace to hearts for 2,000 years. Why don't you try it for your healing, today?

"THE CHRISTIAN'S INSPIRED REVELATION"

I Corinthians 2:9-16

INTRODUCTION:

Many of the greatest minds of the past centuries have spoken upon this subject and by using their human genius have tried to solve the "riddle" of the Bible. On his own, man can go only as far as the five senses, and then his life ends in a plot six feet by about three feet in the "Silent city of the dead." "Whatever is under the sun is vanity." Man has found it so in his unaided search for God. It is this inadequacy that has precluded voyages of discovery into the realm of the Spiritual. In dealing with the Bible, we must conclude that it came from some source outside of man, and that its contents give evidence that it came from God.

PROPOSITION: *Let us examine this Divine revelation.*

I. IT IS IMPOSSIBLE FOR THE BIBLE TO BE THE INVENTION OF MAN.
   A. Not one man of the flesh had ever seen the material contained in the Bible relative to God and man. Vs. 9
   B. Not one man of the flesh had ever heard of the wisdom revealed in this book. Vs. 9
   C. Not one man of the flesh ever had such an understanding of the will of God for man. Vs. 9
   D. Isa. 64:4 It was so from the beginning of the world.
      1. The world, by its wisdom, knew not God. 1:21

II. THE BIBLE IS A REVELATION FROM GOD.
   A. "But God hath revealed them unto us." Vs. 10
      1. Only God, could reveal the mysteries of the sufferings of His Son. Romans 11:33 + John 3:16
      2. The glory of the gospel is that its message is as true and wonderful as the Gracious God who gave it. Gal. 1:12

III. OF WHAT DOES THIS REVELATION CONSIST?
   A. It is the unveiling of the mystery of Christ crucified. Vs. 2.
   B. The great points of importance in this revelation to lost man are:
      1. Christ died for our sins.
      2. He arose from the dead for our justification.
      3. He is coming again to deliver us to God. Heb. 9:26 + I Thess. 4:13-18
   C. It is a revelation of the unbounded Grace of God toward man. Eph. 2:8-9 +; Gal. 1:6; Titus 2:11
   D. It is an all sufficient message. Heb. 7:25.
      1. It is sufficient for this world and for that which is to come.

IV. HOW IS THIS REVELATION MADE KNOWN TO US?
   A. It was by the Spirit's revelation. Vs. 10
   B. It was given to prepared and chosen men; (John 16:4-13. + I Cor. 2:10-11) and that by Revelation from God.
   C. The Holy Spirit is the minister of the things of Christ. I Cor. 12:8-11.
      1. To the Apostles and "Apostolic men" God gave His message of salvation via the crucified Christ!

V. HOW IS THIS DIVINE REVELATION PROCLAIMED?

A. It was proclaimed by words, but not by words only. Vs. 4

1. Accompanying it was the power to demonstrate in the Holy Spirit. (Witness miracles abundant in Paul's Ministry.)

B. God knew that unbelieving man would need to have the message verified, so He equipped His witnesses. Heb. 2:1-4.

C. The combining of spiritual things with spiritual words, only the Spirit of God could have given. Vs. 13

VI. HOW IS THE CHRISTIAN TO REGARD THIS DIVINE REVELATION?

A. Paul expected them to receive it. Vs. 2

B. Paul expected them to reverence it above any prevalent man-made philosophy or any that would ever be invented.

1. Only this revelation suffices for man's salvation.
2. Human philosophies have done nothing except degrade man in the finality. Gal. 1:8-9 + Rev. 22:18-19

C. Paul knew the degrading nemenclatures that men would place upon this message from heaven. "Too narrow"-- "Impractical" etc.

D. God knew and expressed through Paul that it is the wisdom of God to offer this Divine remedy for all the world's woes. Rom. 1:16-17

At Raiatea, one of the Society Islands, six hundred children were assembled at a feast. They marched through the settlement in procession, dressed in pretty dresses, little hats, and bonnets made by parents, who under their former pagan religion, would have destroyed them. The appearance of the parents was most affecting; the eyes of some were beaming with delight. One father said to his wife, "What a mercy it is that we spared our little girl." Bitter tears flowed down the sad faces of others, telling of the painful memory of those they had destroyed.

Finally, a venerable old chief could bear it no longer. He arose, and with an impassioned look and manner, cried, "Let me speak, I must speak. Oh, if I had only known that the Gospel was coming, my children might have been among this happy group; but, alas! I shall die childless, though I have been the father of nineteen children." Sitting down he gave vent to his agonized feelings in a flood of tears.

My friend, physical death that we could have prevented is a terrible thing to remember, but how much worse for men and women all over the world who have heard the message of Salvation--the Divine Revelation for salvation--but have turned it down.

In turning from God they have destroyed themselves, and their own children.

If you have heard this blessed God-sent message you know of salvation by the blood of Christ. For your own sake and the sake of those that come after you, accept it today. Our only hope of the "Place Christ has gone to prepare" is in this divinely inspired message delivered to us by Inspired men.

"WHAT IS NEW IN THE NEW DISPENSATION?"

I Corinthians 2:9

INTRODUCTION:

This scripture, at least in gist, is a quotation from Isaiah 64:4. Often Jewish theologians did not quote verbatim but gave the thought of the verse in differently arranged words. They often modified the thought with other thoughts from the same book or writer. Improperly, this verse is often used to give elaborate descriptions of heaven as imagined by some great preacher, but this can only be done by isolation of verse nine. When the two verses are left as Paul gave them, it is plainly teaching that some glory has been revealed and is now realized by his readers. God dealt with former people, such as Adamic, Patriarchal, Mosaic, Judges, United Kingdom, Divided Kingdom, and the Exilic and Post Exilic periods or ages. Here Paul expressed the thought that we are now in the grandest, most glorious dispensation of all.

PROPOSITION: *How is this Dispensation really NEW?*

I. CHRISTIANITY IS NEW IN THAT IT IS A NEW LIFE, AND NOT NEW CEREMONIES.
   A. This was so new to the Jews it bewildered them. John 3:3-5
      1. Religion was inseparably linked to a system of rituals.
         a. They knew of circumcision, feasts, washings and cliques.
   B. This was new to the Corinthians. II Cor. 5:17
   C. It was new also to the Romans. Rom. 6:4
   D. The Idolater associated religion with esoteric and ceremonial cleansing rituals.
   E. The ultimate then was to try to connect the rituals with the inner man's activities and soul's well being.

F. Here the system is reversed. Because of the new life from God the individual repents of his sins, confesses his faith in the Saviour and is baptized for the remission of his sins. Every ritualistic semblance was based upon the life from God.

II. A GOD-GIVEN SACRIFICE, OFFERED WILLINGLY, WAS NEW TO THE WORLD.

A. In Judaism and all other religions, man must bring the offering.

1. The temple "Business" was carried on in buying and selling sacrificial animals. John 2:13-16
2. Each man had to bring his own sacrificial beast. Lev. 1:2-3

B. Glory is to blossom out of shame; a sublime mission is to be accomplished out of seeming failure.

1. The death of Christ was to bring life to all man-kind. He is the lamb God furnished. John 1:29

C. Christ is to be a new moral force.

1. The Christ who gave Himself so willingly is going to make new creatures out of those who willing give themselves to Him.

III. THROUGH THE DEATH OF CHRIST THE HOLY SPIRIT CAME TO PRODUCE HOLINESS OF LIFE.

A. This was previously unheard of for the mere worshipper.

1. Now, we live by the power within, not struggling in our own strength against insurmountable odds, wherein all men had failed. Rom. 8:1-11 + 14
2. He is the invisible power that lives within every New Creature, giving him victory in every day life. Acts 5:32

B. The Christian knows that if God is with him, no one can successfully stand against him.

IV. THERE IS A NEW TEMPLE NOW IN MAN. I Cor. 6:19

A. Always before there were distinct places where God was supposed to dwell. (Jerusalem, Mt. Sinai, Pillars of fire and shekinah.)

B. God dwelt in Christ demonstrating that He can also live in us. John 14:9-10 "Christ in you the hope of Glory." Col. 1:27; Rom. 8:10

These were all new phases of God's revelation to man. The fullest of them all surpassed in grandeur, power and duration any thing man had ever known before about God. No wonder He says, "Eye hath not seen, ear heard not, and which entered not into the heart of man the GLORIOUS THINGS of God prepared for them that love Him."

To hew a block of marble from the quarry, and carve it into a noble statue—to break up a waste wilderness, and turn it into a garden of flowers—to melt a lump of iron-stone, and forge it into watch springs—all these are mighty changes. Man has done these things throughout the ages, but they all come short of the change which every child of Adam requires. They are merely the same thing in a new form; the same substance in a new shape. Man requires the grafting in of that which he has not had before. He needs a change as great as a resurrection from the dead. He must become a new creature; old things must pass away, and all things must become new. He must be born anew. This is made possible through the message of the "new" covenant.

Our opportunities are superior to those afforded people who lived before Christ; therefore our responsibilities are also greater. When you have heard this message once, God demands "Ye must be born again." If one is not born again, he can not enter heaven. Every man can obey the gospel and be born again, and if he is, he has a place prepared for him by the Lord of the New covenant. Choose the new way brother. Don't miss heaven when God has opened the way for you by Christ!

"TWO NATURES OF MAN COMPARED"

I Corinthians 2:14-15

INTRODUCTION:

When we look about us, we see certain inevitable classifications we must make of men according to their constitutions. The strong, vigorous person, on one hand, never knows what it is to have pain; while on the other hand we see the sick, pale, and feeble ones whose bodies are wracked with pain. There are those who grasp ideas with lightning rapidity, while others could not see the light if it came in lightning flashes. In our classification or comparison here, we are especially interested in those who are spiritual and those who are carnal. Religion appeals to the Spiritual part of man, but on the other side there are those who are merely psychical, physical and intellectual, to whom Christ has no appeal.

These two varieties of men, the Spiritual and the Physical or Natural, have always been recognized by Christianity.

PROPOSITION: *How do they compare?*

I. THE COMPARATIVE SPHERES IN WHICH THEY OPERATE.
  A. Most of their activities move in the same spheres.
    1. They both have a physical sphere—a body, and material creation.
    2. They both have a social sphere—people.
    3. They both have a intellectual sphere—their minds.
  B. The natural man has limitations reaching only to the intellect.
    1. He may be superior in science, literature or the arts, but that is his limit also.
    2. He can not pass beyond the intellectual perceptions which he shares with animal creation.
    3. Pure intellect, reason, and natural affections are his limit.
      a. He has a wide field in which to work.
        (1) Art has yet to reach its perfection.
        (2) The possibilities of knowledge are not exhausted by any means.
  C. We would not minimize the Natural man's sphere, but the Spiritual man enters a realm utterly unknown to the natural man and unknowable as long as he remains the Natural man, alone. John 3:3 "Cannot see...."
    1. It is the sphere of the invisible, everlasting and Spiritual.
    2. He is interested in the things of God. II Cor. 5:17
    3. By regeneration he has been awakened to Divine and eternal things that he never perceived before. (Christian experience)
    4. He has been endowed by God with new senses of perception that he never knew before. II Cor. 12:1-6
    5. Here he finds satisfaction for his full powers that can be found no other place. II Cor. 12:7-10
    6. This greater Spiritual sphere actually encircles all the other spheres, which he shares with the Natural or Carnal man, giving greater meaning to all of them. II Cor. 6:3-10 Phil. 4:11

II. COMPARE THE BEHAVIOUR OF THE TWO.

a. the natural man by his very nature seeks to please himself.
   1. He lends himself to bodily indulgences, although he may learn self-control to meet the standards of society.
   2. His cultural background will have much to do with how far he goes.
   3. Always there is the tendency for bodily passions: lusts, cravings and covetings.
      a. He lives for the enjoyment of the flesh, and appetites. (Witness Herod the Great)

B. The Spiritual man recognizes the lordship of God and his allegiance to Him.
   1. He recognizes the very life he possesses is from God. Gen. 1:26
   2. His body was given to him by God. Gen. 2:7
   3. The world he moves in belongs to God by right of creation. Gen. chpt. 1.
   4. His chief concern is "Am I well pleasing to God?"
   5. He seeks to make his conduct harmonious with God's wishes!
   6. His pathway is ever upward to greater achievements, thus giving him buoyancy of life and higher goals.
   7. His sky is high, as he ever sees the vast pure heavens above beckoning him on and upward.

III. THEIR DESTINIES COMPARED.

A. The natural man thinks only of "Time."
   1. He must "Make it" today, for soon he will pass from all he knows—time, earth, and flesh.
   2. His limitations are here and now, with no future hope.

B. The Spiritual man is concerned with eternity, thinking of this life as only a "Curtain raiser" for the "Main event."
   1. This life is a front porch to the eternal mansions Christ has gone to prepare for him. John chpt. 14.
   2. He realizes the transitoriness of this fleshly life.
      a. As he sees the body weaken, and the physique deteriorate, he is sustained by the Heavenly promise of an "ETERNAL tabernacle." II Cor. 5:1-2

The message of Salvation comes to the world of "Carnal", "Natural" men beckoning them to come up higher and receive from God that Spiritual life promised by the very Son of God, who went through the grave victorious and who has promised the same victory to His "Begotten again children". The gospel given by the Spirit of God is His method of bringing Spiritual life to the fleshly minded men. It is possible for every man to be born again. Mark 16:15-16; Rev. 22:17

An Admiral of the United States Navy, a typical carnal man who had become an authority of sea power and the author of "THE INFLUENCE OF SEA POWER ON HISTORY," came into a small church while in port in Boston. The preacher, in the midst of his sermon, lifted up his hands and quoted Matthew's gospel, "Thou shalt call his name Jesus; for he shall save his people from their sins." The Admiral was stricken in the heart. He said to himself, "Almost the first words of the first gospel and I have not seen them through the years." Scales seemed to fall from his eyes as he turned to follow this new life, to become a Spiritual man rather than remaining a carnal man.

"THE MIND OF CHRIST"

I Corinthians 2:11-16

INTRODUCTION:

Surely there is a vast difference between the natural man and the one who has the mind of Christ. One is not enlightend by the Holy Spirit, the other is; one sees the beauty of Christianity, the other sees only folly; one has the mind of Christ, the other has the attitude of the world; one discerns the beauty of the God-given salvation, the other lives in unmixed darkness. How could two people be more opposite than the man who has the mind of Christ and the man who lives only for physical and material things all his earthly life?

PROPOSITION: *The mind of Christ and its relationship to us.*

I. WHAT DID PAUL MEAN BY "THE MIND OF CHRIST?"
   A. "The mind of Christ" was revealed to us throughout His entire earthly ministry.
      1. His Godly counselling, His promises to the immediate Apostles and to us, and His willingness to sacrifice Himself for us, all reveal that mind.
      2. Surely as we read the Gospels we can not help but say that His mind has come to mean the richest possession that men have today.

B. The mind of Christ was the truth. John 14:6.
   1. He was the truth of God revealed. cf. John 1:14.
C. The mind of Christ loved only the good.
   1. He is the good shepherd. John 10:11
   2. He appealed to his good works. John 10:32
   3. His goodness was reckoned to be God. Matt. 10:17
D. The mind of Christ always chose what was right. Matt. 20:4
   1. He commended the young man for his right choice. Luke 10:28
   2. He promised the righteous should stand forth. Matt. 13:43
E. The mind of Christ chose to suffer for lost humanity.
   1. "Having loved his own that were in the world, He loved them unto the end." John 13:1
   2. He said He would lay down His life for them. John 6:51
   3. He gave His life a ransom for many. Mark 10:45

II. HOW CAN WE POSSESS THE MIND OF CHRIST?
   A. When we consider the greatness of the mind of Christ it makes us almost despair of ever possessing it, yet He has made provision for His children to share in that mind of deity.
      1. The knowledge of the mind of Christ comes to us through the study of the Gospel records.
         a. His mind reveals His plan to save the world; His words, miracles and conduct led to His suffering.
         b. Meditating on these events in His life, we come near to the mind of Christ revealed there.
      2. By faith in His word we come to accept His all sufficient redemption for mankind. John 3:36
         a. He is more than the great example, teacher and revealer of the mind of God; He is our only Saviour. John 14:6
         b. The new life we receive upon our obedience to that form of doctrine, gives us the mind of Christ. Rom. 6:5

III. HOW CAN WE PROVE TO THE WORLD THAT WE HAVE THE MIND OF CHRIST?
   A. By our attitude toward those things that are Spiritual in preference to the material enticements. Rom. 8:4-11
   B. By showing others that we are like Him.
      1. Phil. 2:4-8 "taking the form of a servant..."

The mind of Christ can only be ours when we have been born again. This new birth is based upon faith that comes by the word of Christ. Immediately when God has begotten us into that new life we become "Christ-like", because we have received the embryonic mind of Christ in us, that will grow until we become full grown men and women in Him.

There was at one time in Italy an old sculptor who had, among many other pieces of work in his workshop, the model of a beautiful cathedral. It was covered with the dust of the years. No one admired or paid any attention to it, although it was the exact model, inside and out of one of Europe's finest cathedrals. One day the old attendant placed a light inside the model, and its gleams shone through the beautiful stained-glass windows. Now everyone stopped to admire the model in all its beauty. The change was wrought by the light within; it was marvelous!

It is so with us when Christ comes to dwell in us, and the mind of Christ begins to shine forth from us, then the world sees our good works and glorifies our Father who is in heaven.

"CARNAL CHURCH MEMBERS"

I Corinthians 3:1-4

INTRODUCTION:

Corinth was a great commercial center and, as usual, it was also a center of worldly pleasures and indulgences. Here men worshipped the "Dollar" and drank deep from the fountain of pleasure. They were living in the lap of luxury, but it led them to wallowing in the mire of vice. They worshipped at the magnificent temple of Aphrodite where there were dedicated a thousand sanctified temple harlots. Theaters with burnished exteriors and burning interiors decorated the city. Athletes from all over the world came to Corinth to compete in the Isthmian games. These, plus many other material seductions, combined to make Corinth the "Sodom and Gomorrah" of Greece.

PROPOSITION: *It is no wonder then that Paul speaks of "Carnality" in this letter and how it had invaded the church, the Sanctuary or household of the Holy God.*

I. THE DESCENDANTS OF THESE CARNAL MEMBERS HAVE CURSED THE CHURCH THROUGHOUT THE AGES AND THEY ARE BEARING EVIL FRUIT IN OUR OWN DAY.

A. If they have ANY of the Spirit of Christ, it is certain that He is not dominant in them.
   1. Paul's appeal in Rom. 6:12-14 would be applicable to them.
B. The things of the flesh dominate the Carnal church member.
   1. "Lusts of the flesh and the vain glory of life." I John 2:15-17
C. The world has much attraction to them and wields much power over them.
D. They profess to love the Lord who died for them, but not enough to love the things "above" more than the things "below."
E. They are known for their miserable failures as Christians; their lives are filled with faults.
F. They went through the Bapistry; but they come out "all wet", and not "all filled" with the Holy Spirit.
G. They may be giants in the world, but they are pygmies in the church.

II. HOW DOES PAUL LOOK UPON THEM?

A. He considered them "Babes" when they should have been full grown.
   1. He rebuked them for their infantile condition. Vs. 1-4.
   2. They were useless parasites on the body when they should have been assisting others to grow up.
   3. They were weak; they did not work.
B. Babies require much attention.
   1. The mother church nursing a group of babies hinders her evangelistic efforts.
   2. Often they do not realize they are babies and that adds to the problem.
      a. Correcting a child who thinks he is grown up is a chore.
   3. They are usually unstable and ignorant of the things of God.
   4. Whatever they try to do, is done so poorly that it is a shame to the cause of Christ.
      a. Usually it has to be done over, if it is not entirely ruined by their trial effort.
   5. A child that does not grow up is a source of worry and sorrow to his parents, brothers and sisters.

C. They are unsatisfactory to Christ who bought them, to God who is their Father, and to those with whom they are family members.
1. They destroy all the joy of any public service by their childlishness.
a. Usually those who are so babyish they can not do anything, become sore spots in the church, criticizing everyone else for doing anything.
b. Their fussing spirit soon spreads to the whole congregation.
c. They have not enough religion to be happy in church and too much to just cut loose and raise the Devil, so they are unhappy in both places.
d. They are the promoters of the amusement program of the church today.
(1) They must have parties, weiner bakes, swims, breakfasts, dinners, silver teas, quilting bees, horse back rides, TV, a "coffee break" between Sunday school and church, time to smoke before the communion service and afterwards they go home advertising their "infancy".

D. They can not be reasoned with any more than one can reason with a baby.
1. Usually they think they are the "Smartest of the Smart" and no one can tell them anything.

III. HOW CAN THE CHURCH KNOW IT IS MADE UP OF CARNAL MEMBERS?
A. Examine their fruit.
1. If they are filled with jealousy and strife all the time, you can know they are Carnal.
2. If they always want their own selfish way, they are to be labeled Carnal.
3. If they have a chip on their shoulder and always in a fuss, they are Carnal.
4. If they are producing the fruits of the flesh, (Gal. chp. 5) they are Carnal.
5. If they are unable to assimilate strong meat and always are always griping about the preaching, they are Carnal.

Paul met this situation in Corinth by feeding them "baby food". This must have been humiliating to them especially when this letter was to be read to all the other churches. This gives us a key as to how we are to deal with Carnal Church members.

Begin where they are in their infancy and try by feeding them what they can take—to help them grow up in Christ, to become full grown men and women in the Lord.

The most effective way to deal with this carnal baby church member situation is to make sure people are really "Born Again". By the life from God within, they will grow up readily into strong men and women of the Faith.

Fond parents often have photos taken of their children every month. At the end of the year, they have them made into a composite so they can see the growth of the children over the past year. Suppose the Lord should make such photographic memorials of each one of us? Would we be ashamed of our Infantile condition, or would we be glad for the manifest grown seen by all around us? Would we be spiritual or Carnal?

"LOOKING BACK ON A GRAND EXAMPLE"

I Corinthians 3:1-8

INTRODUCTION:

There is a transcendent power in example. Men trust their eyes more often than they do their ears. We are all an example to someone. People seldom improve when they are surrounded by poor examples. Nothing is so infectious as an example. Noble examples stir us to noble actions. In this scripture we have some examples that can profit all followers of Christ.

PROPOSITION: *Paul and his dealing with the Corinthians, is our example.*

I. FIRST, WE HAVE THE EXAMPLE OF HOW THE TRUTH WAS DISPENSED BY AN APOSTLE.
   A. Paul did not feed all people the same diet. 3:1-2
      1. We must take people where we find them and begin there to build them up in Christ.
         a. We do not teach first graders calculus or how to use the slide rule. Paul taught the Jailor first to believe.
      2. Men could live on meat, but strong meat would kill the young infant. So Paul carefully prescribed.
      3. Jesus did not begin His teaching by introducing the cross.

a. When His disciples had been prepared for the final message, they could receive it. John 16:12.

4. Peter could not understand the Atoning death of Christ, and trying to turn Christ aside, he was told to "Get thee behind me, Satan." Matt. 16:22-23.

B. This example should teach us that a minister may be successful in reaching one class of people and fail miserably with another.

1. Paul at Ephesus was a success and the same Paul at Athens, a failure.

C. We can learn from this example that if we are ever to receive the "Meat of the Word" we must prepare our minds for it, and "Grow up in Christ." "Seek the mind of Christ!"

II. THE SECOND EXAMPLE IS THAT WHICH PAUL HAD TO CONTEND WITH IN THE CHURCH.

A. I Cor. 3:3-4. Envy, strife, jealousy and carnality in general was among the people.

B. They had the embryo of modern denominationalism and sectarianism which we see born and full grown.

1. The divisions have become "Parties" now!

C. Following after men has been the curse of professed followers of Christ, even from the very beginning. I Cor. 1:1-13

D. Creeds, (the crystalization of man's opinions) have become the working hypothesis of each individual opposing sect.

E. Paul said it was "Carnal" then, and it is even more "Carnal" now, for we know the sin of it much better than they.

1. It causes men to trust in the temporal, rather than the eternal; in the "Man-made", rather than the "God-made"; and in the local, rather than the Universal power of the Gospel.

III. THE EXAMPLE OF MINISTERS WORKING TOGETHER AS A TEAM.

A. They were "Ministers through whom ye believed." Vs. 5-7

1. The one who planted was on the same team with the one who watered; each helped the other succeed.

B. Each of these men was different from the other in ability, temperament, education, culture and attainments; yet they supplemented each other; they did not oppose each other!

C. They had one goal, the saving of souls for the building up of the kingdom of God.
   1. They worked as a unit.
   2. Different kinds of labor, but to one end or objective.
D. You will notice they were all under one Master, the Lord.
   1. One Captain ruled their activities for Christ, and He gave the increase.
E. All of them labored together for one eternal and final goal.
   1. The rewards will be meted out at last. Vs. 8; Vs. 14

This example has come from one of God's greatest servants; but we do not have to be an Apostle Paul to be an example, nor to follow an example. I heard of a preacher who visited in a large Colored church in the Mid-eastern part of the United States. It was an "Open meeting" and several of the folk stood up and gave their testimony. Among them was an elderly man who said something the preacher never forgot. He said that as a boy he had gone to Hampton Institute, and had studied hard for six years. At the graduation exercises his most beloved professor said, "Charles, I want you to go out and show what Hampton Institute has done for a poor colored boy."

God's word says, "Quit ye like men; be strong!" Why? Because we are an example to someone. We are showing the world what the Lord Jesus Christ has done for a poor lost sinner, and we want to lead others to the One who has blest our lives.

You are leading some one today! Which way are you leading them?

"THE ONE TRUE FOUNDATION OF CHRISTIANITY"

I Corinthians 3:10-15

INTRODUCTION:

Here Paul changes his figurative language from a garden to the construction of a building. This building like most buildings is composed of many different kinds of material. Every building of value is built according to the architectural design, having one plan from the laying of the foundation to the final super-structure. Every building of importance is designed for a specific purpose. So the Kingdom of God, the Church of Christ on earth, is built by a designer, designed for a specific purpose and is being built by Christians every day.

PROPOSITION: *The foundation of Christianity and the progress of the building.*

I. TRUE CHRISTIANITY HAS BUT ONE FOUNDATION AND THAT IS CHRIST.

   A. Peter was not sufficient foundation for the eternal kingdom of God. Matt. 16:23.
      1. Peter's statement: I Peter 2:4-8 and Acts 4:11-12. He confessed Christ to be the rock.

   B. Christ was spoken of as "a spiritual rock." I Cor. 10:4
      1. Jesus quoted Psa. 118:22-23 and applied it to Himself. "The stone which the builders rejected is become the head stone of the corner." cf. Matthew 21:42; I Peter 2:7

   C. Paul referred to Isa. 28:16 and tells how some people would treat this Christ of God, the Stone He laid.
      1. They stumbled and were offended at it, BUT He says, "he that believeth on him should not be put to shame." Rom. 9:33

   D. The Old Testament made many prophecies and allusions to that Rock foundation that was to come, the Messiah.
      1. Psa. 11:3; 18:15; 27:1; 61:2-3; 62:6-9; 77:14-15; Isa. 28.16
      2. "On Christ, the solid Rock I stand, all other ground is sinking sand."

II. PAUL KNEW MEN WOULD BRING BOTH GOOD AND BAD MATERIALS TO PUT INTO THE BUILDING. Vs. 12,13

   A. Materials such as gold, silver and precious stones build eternally; while wood, hay and stubble only appear to be acceptable building materials.

   B. Some people, like the different types of ground, are worthless, (Matthew 13:19-23) while some are valuable.
      1. Some we thought were converted to Christ, later turned out to be converted to some person.
      2. Some claim to have accepted Christ, but in reality only accepted a creed about Christ; they have a formula, but no change.
      3. Some who went through the form of being born again, were not begotten of God; the new life from God was not evident in them.
      4. Some shouted and made a big scene when they publicly accepted salvation, but it was only a show; there was no visible fruit.
         a. These are hay, wood and stubble.

C. Every preacher has some of each variety.
   1. The New Testament speaks of those Faithful brethren who remained steadfast and immovable.
   2. It also speaks of Demas and those who could not be turned again to the Lord. Heb. 6:4-8

III. THERE IS A FINAL "FIRE TEST" TIME COMING FOR EVERYONE.
   A. Then, every man's work will be made manifest. Vs. 13
      1. Often times now, the large numbers that some GREAT preachers boast of and report, blind our eyes to the fact that there is going to be a FIRE TEST one of these days that will tell the truth about the materials used to build these "Show Palaces."
   B. In that day the Lord will separate the sheep from the goats.
      1. There will be no deception nor show then; the truth will come to light; hypocrisy will be deleted. Matt. 25:31-46
   C. That day will humiliating to those who have built on hay, wood and stubble.
      1. They will suffer loss of "Brotherhood position" in the "100 a year baptism club."
      2. They may be saved themselves, but the vast majority of their building will be burned up in the conflagration.
   D. That day will be a grand and victorious day to those who have carefully built out of genuinely converted men and women. Matt. 13:31-32
      1. They will be rewarded for time spent and talents used in the will of God. Matt. 25:19-23
      2. They will hear "Well done, thou good and faithful servant." The reward given to those who have brought gold, silver and precious stones into the building.

Every preacher is like the bugler sounding the warning. From the steeple of St. Mary's church in Cracow, Poland, a bugle has been sounded every day for the last seven hundred years. The last note on the bugle is always muted and broken, as if some disaster had befallen the bugler. This seven-hundred-year commemoration is in memory of a heroic bugler who one night sounded a blast on his bugle and summoned the people to defend their city against the hordes of the invading Tartars.

As he was sounding the last blast on his bugle, an arrow from one of the Tartars struck him in the neck and killed him.

Every preacher is like that bugler, if he is a faithful man of God. Some day the last note of his warning blast will be blown and then he will stand before the great Captain of our salvation to receive his reward. Then he will be glad that he hewed to the line and brought men and women into the Kingdom genuinely converted, because they are the gold, silver and precious stones that bring the eternal reward. God grant that we will be in that number, when the saints go marching in.

"THE TRUE TEMPLE OF GOD"

I Corinthians 3:16-17

INTRODUCTION:

In the preceeding verses the Apostle has spoken of the church as being a building, but here he says, "Ye are the TEMPLE of God." Naturally the most outstanding feature of the Temple is its sacredness. The one element that made the Corinthian church the temple of God was the fact that the HOLY Spirit abode in them; because of His presence they were to be a HOLY people. This holiness begins in the individual, (any man) and permeates the whole church making it, as a unit, the temple of God. The temple in Jerusalem had been sanctified to God's service. The true temple of God, His church, is also dedicated to the service of God in its highest form. The temple in Jerusalem was located in ONE place, but the true temple of God now is wherever Christians assemble.

PROPOSITION: *Features Paul speaks of, relative to the True Temple of God.*

I. NOTICE THE MATERIAL USED IN ITS CONSTRUCTION.
  A. It was constructed of people. "Ye, are a temple of God." Vs. 16
    1. This is applicable to every Christian in every congregation.
      a. cf. I Peter 2:5 where Peter corroborates this doctrine.
    2. Each member is a stone, built upon the Foundation, filling its appointed place in the spiritual building. (Temple)
  B. Christ was the master architect in this building procedure.
    1. It was His idea that Spiritual temple be built out of Redeemed men and women. It is a concept worthy of God.

II. THIS TEMPLE WAS CONSECRATED BY A DIFFERENT PRESENCE.

A. Isa. 60:1-2 speaks of the Glory of God shining, or the "Presence of God" which was in the Holy of Holies in the Old Testament tabernacle.

1. The word Shekina does not appear in the Bible, but it means the Glorious one; His presence.

B. This Temple, made up of people who have the Holy Spirit dwelling in them, becomes the place where the SPIRIT DWELLS.

1. His presence is seen in every "Stone" in the Temple.

a. He has transformed them, given them life, filled them with purified power, and consecrated each one of them. It literally "Glows with the light of His presence."

b. Ancient kings had their names on every brick in their buildings.

III. WHAT IS THE ORDER OF WORSHIP IN THE TEMPLE OF CHRIST?

A. From it and through it are proclaimed the living oracles of God.

B. The sacrifices are continual praises to God. Heb. 13:15

1. The hearts of the people produce psalms, hymns and spiritual songs. Col. 3:16-17

2. The prayers of the Saints are the incense in this temple. cf. Rev. 5:8 + 8:3

3. The blood washed Saints give eternal adoration to the Lord who redeemed them; not at certain times of the year, or once a week, but always, continually.

IV. WHAT ONE TERM CAN BE USED TO DESCRIBE THIS TEMPLE?

A. Vs. 17 "For the temple of God is Holy." It is made holy by the blood of Christ, and kept holy by the Holy Spirit.

1. This is not acquired by ceremonial cleansing.

a. The cleansing INSIDE that shows forth through the external man in his association with man and women of the world. "Christ liveth in Me!"

2. This holiness of character makes holiness of word and deed. Gal. 5:22-23

V. HOW SHOULD WE REGARD THIS NEW TEMPLE?

A. The temple was entered only by the ones designated of God, and so it is with this one. Only God's "Born again" people can enter. John 3:3-5

B. As the old temple was treated with reverance, so this one should be even more venerated. Universal and eternal!
   1. A king's subjects treat him with respect, and Christians should treat the abode of the Holy Spirit with even greater respect.
   2. "...Ye have your fruit unto sanctification, and the end eternal life." Rom. 6:22

There is a place reserved in Jesus' Temple for every lost soul. A very selfish man once dreamed that he was trying to build a temple to commemorate his own name; he wanted the whole temple to himself. An angel came to show him one that was a model of beauty, but there was one stone missing from its peak. The man asked the angel where it was. "There has never been one there," replied the angel. "We intended to place you there, but you say that you want a whole temple to yourself, so this place will be filled by some one else. But you will never have your special temple."

Then the man, aroused by his fears, started up from his sleep crying, "Oh God, PUT ME IN YOUR TEMPLE! PUT ME IN, EVEN THOUGH I CAN BE ONLY A CHINK STONE. PUT ME IN YOUR TEMPLE, FOR JESUS SAKE."

Oh, sinner friend, will you be awakened to the eternal importance of being in the Holy, Eternal Temple of the Lord, His church? Come in now, while you may!

"WORLDLY WISDOM"

I Corinthians 3:18-20

INTRODUCTION:

The "Wisdom" that Paul refers to here is the same as he spoke of in 1:20. It is "fleshly-wisdom" or "wisdom of the world," "wisdom of this age." It is merely intellectual wisdom as applied to secular things, and as it seeks to apply itself to a religion that is purely of fleshly origin. It is seen in the realm of the philosopher and in the many fake religions that have sprung from the "minds of man," unaided by divine revelation from God. Men say, "Oh, I think this will be alright" or "If I just pay my debts and treat my neighbor right, I'll make it OK"; but God says these things are "fleshly wisdom." They are foolishness with God. Certainly it is self deluding, spiritually worthless, and in the end confounding and soul-damning.

PROPOSITION: *The way of true wisdom, how it is found, and our end if we do not find it.*

I. THOSE WHO POSSESS FLESHLY WISDOM MUST BECOME FOOLS BEFORE THEY CAN ATTAIN GOD'S WISDOM.
  A. Worldly wisdom is useful in making money, buying property, doing mathematical problems; but it is useless when it comes to understanding the mind of God in relationship to man.
    1. Usually the smarter a man thinks he is, the harder it is for him to learn anything from God's revelation.
       He thinks he knows a better way and begins to judge God instead of letting God judge him.
    2. Pride or a "know-it-all-attitude" is a bar to making progress in any field.
       Doctors who thought they knew all the answers could not accept Harvey's demonstration of blood circulation.
    3. We must acknowledge our weaknesses in order to grow stronger; our foolishness in order to become wise in God's sight.
  B. Recognizing our foolishness and God's wisdom is the beginning of our Christian life.
    1. The new birth is foolishness to the worldly-wise man.
       a. How often man's fleshly wisdom hinders him from accepting God's salvation.
       b. They think they know a better way. John 3:3-5; II Cor. 5:17 "Old things must pass away."
    2. Only when the fleshly-wise Paul renounced his Pharisaical heritage and believed on the Lord Jesus, did he find the peace every soul seeks. Acts 22:16
  C. Our progress, in the process of growing in Christ, depends on our accepting God's wisdom in preference to our own.
    1. People have various ideas about how they should grow up. Modern psychology, with its crazy twists, is the product of man's unguided fleshly wisdom.
       a. Attend lodge regularly and treat my "brother lodge members" well.

b. Enter a monastary or nunnery and live a cloistered life separated from all evil.
c. Just be good and kind to everybody.
d. Sleep on a mattress made of sharp nails.
e. All of these men have invented ideas and have tried to grow spiritually, but to no avail.

2. We can grow in patience, spiritual insight, and holiness. We can develop hope and faith by esteeming ourselves foolish and by accepting the inspired teachings from God recorded in the Bible.

II. LOOKING AT MAN'S FAILURES, WE SHOULD BE ABLE TO SEE THAT THE WISDOM OF THE WORLD IS FOOLISHNESS WITH GOD.

A. In God's judgment (He will be the final judge.) our wisdom is folly.

1. Man's speculations have brought idolatry into the world, (the height of foolishness) philosophies and religions that have cursed whole continents (India and the whole of Asia).
   a. They contain enough truth to lead people astray and enough poison to kill the whole population.
   b. They are like a beautiful bridge that reaches only half way across a chasm; they fail to reach God.
   c. Those who have given the most time in this research are the first to admit their inadequacy.
2. The worldly-wise men have wrestled with these problems for a life time, and then passed them on unsolved to the next generation. (Witness the whole heathen world.)

B. Look at the concoctions produced by man's so called wisdom in the endeavors to regenerate the world.

1. Education, aesthetic national cultures, various moral standards, Socialism, Communism, Humanism, Unitarianism, Modernism, all have been tried in various sections and been found "wanting!"
2. All have absolutely failed to redeem mankind from his fallen condition and to restore him to his original position before God.

   Men have never been proven so foolish as in the fields where they think they are the wisest. Their wisdom has brought them only foolishness.

Oh, my friend, listen to God! In your fleshly wisdom turn to Him for His eternal and all sufficient wisdom that brought salvation to all by the great sacrifice of His Son, and that will bring our redemption and new life from God. Listen and obey!

McCaulley said: "God, the uncreated, the incomprehensible, the invisible, attracted few worshipers; a philosopher might adore so noble a conception, but the crowd turned away in disgust from words that presented no image to their minds. It was before Deity embodied in human form, working among men, partaking of their infirmities, leaning on their bosoms, weeping over their graves, bleeding on the cross, that the prejudices of the synagogue, and the doubts of the academy, and the pride of the portico, and the fasces of the lictors and the swords of the thirty legions were humbled in the dust."

Christ was the "Foolishness of God" overcoming the "Wisdom of the World."

"OUR RIGHTFUL POSSESSION"

I Corinthians 3:21-23

INTRODUCTION:

A very poor peasant in the old country received a ticket for ship passage to visit his rich relative in the United States. He took the ticket and his little travelling bag and boarded the great ocean liner that was headed for the land of promise. After four days at sea, the chief steward sent one of his men in search for this one passenger who had not come to the dining-table. He went to the man's cabin and knocked on the door. The man inside opened the door just enough to speak through. He was frightend and did not want anyone to know how poor he really was. The steward asked why he had not been to the dining-room, but he merely grunted. Then he was asked if he was sick. He told the inquirer he was well enough and enjoying the trip. Then came the insistent question, "Why have you not been to the dining-room?" No answer, but the steward could see something on a small table that looked like food. He asked if he had been eating in his cabin. The passenger was afraid he had done wrong, so he confessed before he made more trouble for himself. To his utter amazement he learned that all his meals were furnished with the ticket he had in his possession. He had been living on cheese and crackers when the finest food had been prepared for him.

Many Christians are like that. They possess all the blessings recorded in God's gift-list, yet they live as though they were beggars. It is true we should not live above our income in life, but in Christ we should not live BELOW our status in life, either! We have, in Christ, UNSEARCHABLE RICHES!

PROPOSITION: *What has God given to the Christian? Paul says, "all things are yours."*

I. WE HAVE, IN CHRIST, THOSE THINGS THAT ARE REAL AND YET MOVEABLE.

A. The possessions we have in Christ can be taken with us wherever we go.

1. We can share a blessed experience with others anywhere we go.
2. "Peace that passeth understanding"-even jail can not take it away.
   cf. Paul and Silas in jail. Acts chp. 16.
3. "We have joy unspeakable and full of glory." I Peter 1:8
   No one can take it away from us.
4. We have goodness, and righteousness that comes by regeneration, to show forth the Holy Spirit in our lives. Matt. 5:10-11+16
5. We have a love for both friends and foes that the world can not understand. They can not take it from us; it is a glorious gift.
   Stephen showed it in his death. Acts 7:59-60

II. WE HAVE TRUE PREACHERS ON THE EARTH TO HELP US.

A. They are represented here in Paul, Cephas and Apollos. Vs. 22

1. A preacher does not possess the church, but the church does possess the preacher for her own edification.
2. All these preachers belonged to all the Christians in the church there, and everywhere they went.
3. Preachers are proficient in different fields; some plant, some water, and some reap the increase; but they all belong to Christians everywhere.

B. We, as Christians, should rejoice at the blessings God has given us and live up to our privileges.

III. WE HAVE THE WORLD AS OUR SERVANT; IT IS NOT TO BE OUR MASTER.

We as Christians are given every good thing to use to the glory of God, our Father.

1. These good things are not to be used to the detriment of weaker brethren. I Cor. 10:32-33
2. They are used as a gift from God to help others.

IV. WE HAVE LIFE GIVEN TO US AND THE VICISSITUDES OF LIFE SUPERVISED BY A LOVING FATHER. I Peter 2:19-21
A. The world has troubles just the same as we do; but with us, God hallows and sanctifies them to our own good. Rom. 8:28
B. The Christian looks upon a long lingering sickness as a blessing from God in that it gives him time to willingly break the ties that bind him to this earth, and prepare to gladly leave it all behind.

V. WE AS CHRISTIANS ARE GIVEN DEATH, BUT WE MEET IT IN HOPE.
A. II Tim. 4:6-8. To Paul, death was like a ship leaving port to make a voyage into the "Haven of Rest" where our Captain has gone before.
B. We have learned to trust God in life and in death. II Cor. 1:9-10
C. We are determined to glorify Christ in life and in death. Phil. 1:20-23

VI. WE AS CHRISTIANS HAVE THE PROMISE OF A FUTURE LIFE WITH GOD.
A. We have Jesus Christ's word as our future hope. John 6:39-40
B. This life begins in the resurrection. Phil. 3:21
C. It surpasses all efforts to describe the place He has gone to prepare for us. Rev. 21:1-7
We are satisfied to know we shall be in His presence and be like Him. I John 3:2-3

The most advanced Philosophers say that blessedness does not come this side of death, because as long as one is alive there is trouble. The message from God goes farther. It shows a more perfect blessedness than they ever conceived for the next life, and it imparts that blessedness in this life also.

Coleridge, the poet, in a letter written a fortnight before his death, addressed to his child said, "On the eve of my departure, I declare to you, that health is a great blessing; competence, obtained by honorable industry, a great blessing. It is a great blessing to have kind, faithful and loving friends, and relatives; but the greatest blessing, as it is the most ennobling of all privileges, is to be, indeed, a Christian."

Why? Because we have all things good now, and the promise of better things in eternity for which we earnestly strive.

"THE DEVIL OF DIVISION"

I Corinthians 3:21-23

INTRODUCTION:

Three factions had arisen among the followers of Christ in Corinth. At first they had all been "of Christ," but now they were of Paul, Apollos, and Cephas, dividing the Body which is the church. Apparently it was not the fault of the preachers, but rather the fault of men who divided the followers into these groups; men who thought they were wise in their own conceits. Paul did not encourage their disunity but rather rebuked them. If biting words could wound, this would have been a battlefield infirmary. Division always works destruction to the cause of Christ. Paul wanted them to glorify Christ, so he asks, "Is Christ divided?" Have you cut Him up like a beef and parceled Him out among you? Was Paul crucified for you? No, it was Christ, and they knew it. Paul preached that Christ was made wisdom, righteousness and sanctification unto redemption in their presence.

Partisanship hinders spiritual progress, placing men ahead of the message from God. So Paul urged them to put down personal rivalries in the Church.

PROPOSITION: *The cause and cure of divided brethren in the church.*

I. WHAT USUALLY CAUSES DIVISION AMONG THE FOLLOWERS OF CHRIST?

Pride is possibly the greatest cause of partyism. Prov. 21:4

1. Pride of knowledge. ("Brother KNOW-IT-ALL.") I Cor. 8:1
   - a. He knows who is right and who is wrong. I Tim. 3:6
   - b. He knows what has to be done and how to do it.

c. He knows better than God what the organization of the church should be like.
d. His wisdom is far superior to Deity in fixing the qualifications of the elders and deacons.

2. Pride of power. ("I rule'm or ruin'em.") Jer. 13:15
   a. He must be the chairman of the committee.
   b. He must be advisor to the ladies council, that he has organized.
   c. He must be on the pulpit supply committee, and building committee; his advice must be sought on whatever they intend to do, or he is mad.
3. Pride of place or position.
   a. He has "it made." Wealthiest member!
   b. He has proven his superiority in all fields.
   c. He is recognized as a leading citizen, and accomplished in his field, so he should be recognized in ALL fields.
   d. Because of his "Position" all men should follow him, but usually he succeeds only in causing "Splits" in the church.
   e. The larger the split, the larger becomes his egotism.
   f. He acts like the "Buck" in a herd of deer; boss to be admired by all his followers.

This party-split is like a skin infection, the more you scratch it the more it spreads, until after a while the whole body is infected. Usually the "skunk that caused the stink" slips out and leaves the silly people who followed him to hold the bag and receive the blame for the trouble. It takes foolish followers as well as proud leaders to make a division in the church.

II. WHAT IS THE CURE FOR THIS AGE-OLD-CURSE OF CHURCH DIVISION?

A. Secure a proper relationship to Christ. Vs. 23
   1. Be loyal to HIM instead of to ANY man in the church.
   2. Place preachers and leaders as servants ONLY of Christ.
   3. Demand that all who lead be loyal to a "Thus saith the Lord."
      a. Even in what God says about "Church dividers."
      b. Demand that they live up to the spirit of the law as well as the letter.
   4. See that a "Christ liveth in me" attitude controls the membership. Gal. 2:20

a. He alone is our Master to follow and obey.
b. Refuse to be named after any man who lives, or who has lived.
c. See that "Love for the brethren" abounds... I Cor. 13:4-7

B. Take everything God gives you through every TRUE preacher of "The Word", but refuse to become a member of any man's "Party."
1. If there are no members, then there can be no party. It is silly followers as well as ungodly leaders that divide the body of Christ. I Cor. 1:12
2. Make a full surrender of ourselves to Christ, and then no other leader will have any opportunity to lead off soldiers after him. John 21:22
3. Have full loyalty to Christ and His church and true soldiers will recognize the factious rebel leader as soon as he seeks to divide the followers into fussing groups.

Diagnosing a disease is important, but if there is no sure cure prescribed the diagnosis is worthless. Paul prescribes and admonishes in I Cor. 1:10-15.

In one of my meetings in years past I was completely blocked in making any progress by the church being "split right down the middle" into two factions that had lasted for many years. On one side were the Jonesites, on the other the Smithites and woe to the poor unfortunate who got on the wrong side or half-way between, because he would be torn to pieces by the two factions pulling him in opposite directions. The members had done nothing but glare at each other and disgrace the name of Christ for years. During the meeting on a Sunday evening the Spirit of God began to move in their midst and men began to cross over the line and take each other by the hand and apologize. Women began to go to each other and cry in Christian embrace. The ice broke and the sweet Spirit of Christ came into that factious, sin-cursed congregation. Before the meeting closed there were fifty people converted to the Lord. God blesses a united people who love HIM. Disunity is destroyed by Divine love for each other.

"ACCOUNTED AS TRUE MINISTERS"

I Corinthians 4:1-4

INTRODUCTION:

Paul had condemned unmercifully the partisan spirit in the congregation at Corinth. In exposing the division as sin, naturally the ministers enter into the picture. They were divided over their ministerial leadership, wearing their names to their disgrace. His biting words wounded as he informed them that those who destroy the influence of the church and make it useless, God would destroy. Divisions did and still do work destruction to the preacher and to the church. Paul would exalt Christ and thus form the ONLY unifying bond that would last.

PROPOSITION: *What are the characteristics of a good minister and faithful steward of Christ?*

I. A GOOD MINISTER MUST BE A SERVANT OF CHRIST. 3:5
   A. Not ministers of a denomination or a church, but of Christ. 4:1
   B. The church can not strangle the preacher and force him to preach what they desire. He is first a servant of Christ! Salary or "large givers" should not influence his message.
   C. The curse of "State Religion" is that the state thinks the preacher should preach to please them. Rome killed Paul.
   D. A true minister does not swerve to the right or the left, but goes straight ahead for his Master. I Tim. 6:3-5 + 20-21
   E. He fearlessly exposes any enemy of God or of His people. Gal. 1:6-8; Phil. 3:2; II Cor. 11:3-4; 13-15

II. A TRUE MINISTER MUST BE A RESPONSIBLE PERSON. "STEWARDS OF THE MYSTERIES OF GOD." A TREMENDOUS RESPONSIBILITY LAYS ON HIS SHOULDERS.
   A. This "Mystery" simply means that the Gospel was not all made known at one time in the past, but has been a gradual REVELATION by chosen, inspired men.
      Ministers are "Stewards" or "Caretakers" of it, and they must be responsible persons.
   B. The Gospel is mystifying at first to the novice, but as time goes on, under the tutelage of a good minister, it becomes clear. II Cor. 4:7; 8:23; Eph. 4:11-12; Col. 4:17

III. A GOOD MINISTER MUST BE DEPENDABLE. "MUST BE FOUND FAITHFUL" Vs. 2
   A. He must be dependable to carry out his commission from God. I Tim. 4:6-7; 12-16; I Tim. 5:17 + 21; I Tim. 6:13-14 + 20-21

B. He is not to turn aside to his own ideas, but "Preach the word." II Tim. 4:2; Titus 2:1 + 7-8 + 15

C. God is the OWNER, and the minister merely acts as His steward. Jas. 3:1 + 13; I Peter 5:3-4; II Tim. 1:13-14; 2:1

IV. A GOOD MINISTER MUST NOT FEAR MAN'S JUDGMENT! 4:3

A. The man of God must know what he is doing and that it is faithful and right before God.

He must go forward though the whole church and world be in array against him. Acts 21:10-14 + 24:24-26

B. It is not the preacher's business to go about trying to make people mad at him by his being stubbornly obnoxious; but if they hate him for being faithful, he is not to swerve. Heb. 13:7-8

V. A GOOD MINISTER MUST BE A FAITHFUL MAN; HAVING A CLEAR CONSCIENCE IN SERVICE.

A. He must continue in the things which he is assured of to be right. II Tim. 3:12-17; II Tim. 4:5

B. He must be faithful to the charge he has taken. II Tim. 1:6 + 13-14

VI. A GOOD MINISTER MUST BE ALWAYS MINDFUL THAT GOD'S JUDGMENT WILL BE RIGHT AND FINAL. II Tim. 4:1

A. The faithful minister has a crown awaiting him. II Tim. 4:8

B. Then the true motives of the minister will be judged. I Cor. 3:13; Rom. 14:10-14. What men have said, will not count then.

C. The true minister depends upon God's judgment to vindicate him and his message, finally. II Cor. 5:10

D. That judgment will be "by the man whom He hath ordained," who is the preacher's Example and Master. Acts 17:30-31

All ministers leave their mark upon the people to whom they minister. The tree is known by its fruit—the preacher is known by his people. Whenever I find it difficult to awaken and arrest the attention of an audience—lolling at their ease, and wearing in their faces an air of dull indifference—I do not need any one to tell me that their usual Sundays have been a weariness—their minister a poor, uninteresting preacher. And much have they to answer for, who, devoting too little time and labor to their sermons, indulge their taste, some for literature, and others for laziness, at the expense of the souls of the people.

A good minister prepares his sermon before he comes to the pulpit and in the pulpit he works on that same sermon, not dilly-dallying around half asleep; but he faithfully proclaims the unsearchable riches of Christ as though men's souls and everlasting lives depended upon his efficacy as their minister.

"HOW TO DEAL WITH VANITY IN RELIGION"

I Corinthians 4:7-8

INTRODUCTION:

Every man has just as much vanity as he lacks in understanding. All other passions have intermissions, but vanity gives no let-up, or respite to its victims. Nothing is so credulous as vanity, nor so ignorant of what is really becoming to itself. Someone has said, "When men will not be reasoned out of vanity, they must be ridiculed out of it."

That is the method Paul used on these proud and vain church members in Corinth. Irony is a method used often in the scriptures. I Kings 13:27; Job 12:2.

PROPOSITION: *Notice Paul's use of flesh-cutting irony in dealing with these vain people. (Irony is saying one thing when you mean exactly the opposite.)*

I. THESE CHURCH MEMBERS, IN THEIR CARNALITY, THOUGHT THEMSELVES TO BE THE VERY SPIRITUAL. PAUL CUTS THEM OFF WITH SATIRE AND IRONY.
   A. They acted as though they were "self-made" men. Vs. 7 "What hast thou that thou didst not receive?"
      1. Every good thing they had, Paul had given to them.
      2. They had only the ungodly elements among them that they had acquired personally.
   B. Paul reproached them ironically, "Now ye are full!"—"Already ye are filled."
      They thought knowledge was complete, but in reality Paul was emphasizing their utter emptiness of the great spiritual qualities it takes to make Christian character.

C. "Now ye are rich..." It was suspiciously early for them to have so attained.
   1. They were wanting in nothing; they had no needs, but rather were affluent.
   2. This was in reality an ironic prodding because of their abject poverty and immaturity in spiritual things. (Note the great sins they possessed as depicted in the later chapters of this book.) cf. Rev. 3:17-19

D. He next says, "Ye have reigned as kings without us;"
   1. No one, in their minds, were as high as they.
      a. They were, in their own eyes, monarchs of all they surveyed.
      b. They had come to this high-ranking position without the assistance of such a lowly personage as the Apostle Paul.
   2. In reality Paul is saying, "you are without the first premise of Christianity—self-sacrifice." Mark 8:34-35 One cannot be a disciple of Christ without this qualification. They were bereft of it.

II. THESE CONCEITED, VAIN CHURCH MEMBERS THOUGHT THEY DID NOT NEED THE HUMBLE SERVICES OF SUCH A ONE AS PAUL. Vss. 18-19

A. Paul dealt with vanity in the most effective way, i.e. satire.

   Sometimes the best manner to deal with the swaggering, self-important, vain man is not to judge him by your judgment of him, but just speak out-loud what he thinks of himself. To speak it is usually enough to deflate him. Rom. 2:4-11

B. They were spoken of as strong, impregnable, triumphant; while the Apostle, who had brought them their salvation, was looked upon as weak, overcome and defeated.

   He had been in their midst, "in weakness and fear, and in much trembling." cf. II Cor. 11:23-30

C. They were, ironically stated, honorable men having dignity; but Paul was despised and despicable.

   Actually, they were in a fool's paradise and Paul was breaking down the glass wall they had built around themselves. II Cor. 11:10-15

This was the condition which caused Paul to have to expose them for what they were. He was trying to pry their eyes open that they might see themselves as they really were.

We should remember that irony and satire are dangerous weapons and not to be used in the hands of the novice. Even the greatest of men are to use it sparingly. If one does not watch himself, he will find irony too pleasant a tool to use. If it is ever used, it must be accompanied with good sound and sober arguments to drive home the lesson desired. Always it should be given in the spirit of love and the desire to rescue and build up the ones addressed in such a manner. 4:14-16 Paul pleads with them as a father, and admonishes them to become imitators of himself.

Thank God, Paul had set a magnificent example of genuine lowliness of mind and willingness to sacrifice himself for their welfare; therefore he could implore them to follow him, and as he later adds, "even as I also am of Christ." I Cor. 11:1

Christ is still seeking genuine followers. Many professed Christians are like the Corinthians; they are too high on the ladder of "SELF" to follow Jesus. They follow Christ like Samson followed his parents, until he came to a beautiful honey-comb or Philistine maiden and then he turned aside. Others follow Jesus like a dog follows his master till he comes across some old dead carcus and then turns aside to wallow in it. Some follow like Demas, who forsook God having gone after this present world, drifting onward and downward until finally he became a priest in an idolatrous temple.

God wants great men who will become small enough to do His bidding. Like the sunflower follows the sun even on cloudy days, tracing its course through the heavens, even when the sun's face is hidden, so God wants men and women to follow Him, not proud but humble followers of the Lord, poor in Spirit but inheriting the earth.

"AN INTER-WORLD SPECTACLE"

I Corinthians 4:9 + Hebrews 12:1-2

INTRODUCTION:

The Greek word theatron is translated "spectacle" from which our word theater comes. This pictorial language, employed by Paul, is readily understood by the people of Corinth for they were in a city of great theatrical spectacles. Usually, theaters were built in the form of an amphitheater where the "stage" was surrounded by a circular seating arrangement. They were immense outdoor theaters seating tens of thousands of spectators. All sorts of attractions were presented there from boxing with mailed fists (often to the death), to the finest of arts and rhetorical contests. Paul says that the Apostles were exposed to the view of all the world, to angels and to men, in the program unto which they were appointed. Actually, the world is a "moral theater" and every person is acting a part, while the world and the angels are constant spectators. This fits not only the Apostles, but every one of us. (Heb. 12:1)

PROPOSITION: *How then should we conduct ourselves in this play?*

I. WE SHOULD REMEMBER THAT OUR CONDUCT CONCERNS HEAVEN AND EARTH.
   A. Our influence is affecting someone, probably many. Rom. 14:7 II Cor. 5:15.
      1. We should strive to be like Paul in Phil. 1:20-21.
      2. Each one of us can be likened to a strand in a hawser; we either strengthen the cause of Christ, or weaken it by our actions.
         "Some one is watching your light." "Oh, does it shine with a radiance bright?"
   B. Angels as well as men are interested in how we live.
      1. We can make angels rejoice, or possibly weep. Luke 15:10
      2. They are interested because they are offsprings of the same God.
      3. They participate in the same nature and are ruled by the same moral government. cf. Jude 6.

II. WE SHOULD DO OUR PART WELL TO PLEASE GOD.
   A. When the "curtain goes up" on the stage, all is business.
      1. The actor goes "all out" to play his part well, inculcating into every action his genius and his acquired cultural art.
   B. We are playing before a large audience composed of people from every walk of life and they all KNOW what is expected of one who professes to be a Christian.
      1. They watch to see if we are a humble acting people. Matt. 5:3
      2. They know we should be hungering and thirsting for righteousness.

They observe whether we are faithful in church attendance where righteousness is dispensed and engendered. Matt. 5:6

3. They are critics of our actions where mercy is involved. Matt. 5:7
4. They listen to our talk, knowing that out of the heart the mouth speaketh. They see whether it is pure. Matt. 5:8
5. If we are presenting Christ by way of faction and causing a stir everywhere we go, they know it. Matt. 5:9
6. They watch to see if we stand up under fire from the persecutor, or whether we look for a milder climate when the "heat is on." Matt. 5:10-11

C. Most of the people of the world know how high God has set the standards and that should call out a strong response in us; but when we remember that the hosts of heaven, pure in the presence of God, are observing us, how meticulously we should play our part on the stage of life.

III. WE SHOULD REMEMBER WE ARE "ON STAGE" AND THERE IS NO PLACE TO HIDE.

A. We cannot hide from God nor from His angels.

They are His "bloodhounds of the sky" and final avengers. Matt. 13:41

B. The world is watching our outward actions, but "God looketh upon the heart," and no thought or deed goes unnoticed. I Sam. 16:7

IV. WE CAN BE SURE GOD WILL NOT DESERT US ON THE STAGE, BUT STANDS ALWAYS READY TO "COACH" US WHEN WE FALTER. I Cor. 10:13

A. God has "ministering spirits" that He uses to assist us. Heb. 1:6-7; Vs. 14

God has plenty of them. Rev. 5:11

B. God has always ministered to His people when they faced trouble.

1. Gideon, Judges 6:11-22
2. David, II Sam. 24:16
3. Daniel, Dan. 6:22
4. Philip, Acts 8:26
5. Paul, Acts 27:33
6. John, Rev. 1:1

Even before we become Christians we wield an influence, and up until we do accept Christ that influence is against our Lord and Saviour. Why not get right with God and come onto the stage as a representative of the Lord to glorify His name?

Our influence is like ointment that betrayeth itself (Prov. 27:16), like sound that spreads far and wide, like the shrill sound of the trumpet (I Thess. 1:8), like leaven gradually infecting the whole mass, like salt preserving and seasoning (Matt. 5:13). Why not get right with God and be a heavenly influence on all the world, in the presence of men and angels, for time and for eternity?

The first act that puts us on stage for God is our accepting Christ as our Saviour. Then Christ directs the play and we must play our part to glorify Him. Be in earnest about life!

When William Lloyd Garrison commenced the publication of the "Liberator," he began it with these memorable words: "I am in earnest—I will not equivocate—I will not excuse—I will not retreat a single inch—and I will be heard." He was heard and the chains have fallen from the three million bondmen to whose service he consecrated his life.

When any person makes up his mind to turn to the Lord, God is waiting to save him from his sins. He will make of him a new creature, enter his name upon the Lamb's book of life and start him on the stage of life for God and for Heaven, to influence men and angels.

"HOW CAN THE TERM FATHER BE PROPERLY USED IN THE CHRISTIAN RELIGION?"

I Corinthians 4:15

INTRODUCTION:

Jesus forbade the use of the word Father as a religious title in Matt. 23:9. From this text in I Corinthians we can observe that Paul is referring to his begetting them in Christ, after the type of a father begetting children in the natural manner. Here paternity is referred to in the spiritual realm. Most men who demand the title of Father are bachelors.

PROPOSITION: *How may we use the word Father properly?*

I. WHAT DOES IT MEAN TO BECOME THE SPIRITUAL FATHER OF ANOTHER PERSON?
   A. It does not mean that we merely give some of our ideas or ideals to some other person.

Every generation produces men of capabilities who can put their ideas across, either by personality or the well-paid press, so that thousands of people think their thoughts after them.

Most school teachers have this ability and the more of it they possess the better teachers they are.

J. F. Kennedy seemed to be having some success in molding the minds of the American public. (God pity us.)

B. It means more than some profound school of thought or method of presenting arguments.
   1. A philosophical movement known as Scholasticism dominated the western church during the Carolingian period.
   2. It was succeeded by Cartesianism which sought to keep faith and philosophy, religion and reason in separate fields.
   3. Newton, who swayed millions, has now been succeeded by Einstein as a leader of men's thoughts; but being a spiritual father to people means more than this molding method of teaching.

C. A Spiritual father tries and partially succeeds in changing men's moral character by instilling in them Christ Jesus, the new life from God.

II. WHAT DOES A CHRISTIAN FATHER PRODUCE IN HIS OFF-SPRING?

He produces a Christ-likeness. He stands in direct contrast to the sensual, selfish and unbelieving characters we meet in our daily lives.

1. Christ living within produces the highest good known to man.
   a. Who can surpass the Spiritual level to which Christ attained and Christians aspire? Gal. 5:22-24; Rom. 12:1-2
   b. When one is born again he has the same Father Christ had. John 3:3-5 tells us we are children of God, begotten from above. Jesus taught his disciples to pray, "OUR Father, who art in heaven......."
2. One begotten again naturally loves the one through whom God does the begetting. I John 5:1
3. There is a genuineness of affection that exists between the one begotten and the father in the new birth, more than there is in the natural birth relationship. Matt. 10:37.

4. When we are begotten of God we love not only our Spiritual father, but we love all others who are begotten of God. I John 5:2-4

   The tender ties of this relationship are seen in Gal. 4:10 and in II Tim. 1:2, "my beloved child." There was a special affection that Paul bore toward his children in the gospel.

III. WHAT METHOD IS TO BE USED TO BEGET THIS CHRIST-LIKE CHARACTER IN OTHERS?

A. Paul says he begat them "through the Gospel." Vs. 15

   The Gospel of Christ is the ONLY method God has given to accomplish the new birth. Rom. 1:16-17

   That is why Jesus said, "Go into all the world and preach the Gospel to every creature."

B. Here, in getting people born again, Judaism, psychology, philosophies and lying on a bed of hot nails fail; creeds, though revised every decade, fail; Mohammedanism and Buddhism also fail.

C. Life from God is transferred to the heart of man via the good news of the death, burial and resurrection of Christ; He comes to live within and He transforms.

   1. It is the Gospel that brings about the "New Birth."
   2. In the process, the father sows the seed of the kingdom, the gospel, in the heart of the one who is to be born again.

Paul says he is their FATHER, and he became so by the gospel; therefore we know it is proper to use the word father in this sense. The new birth makes us more honorable than our first birth, no matter what dignities came with our first birthright. The children of the president have the same blood tainted in Adam as all others, and mingled in all their posterity.

Any person who takes the gospel of Christ to another and causes him to believe and obey the Lord, becomes the spiritual father of that person. This is the highest calling on earth. There is only one person who derives more from the new birth than the one who causes it, and that is the one who is born again. His life is made anew; he enjoys new things. He hates the old things he once revelled in; old habits drop off like frost in a warm refrigerator. He rejoices in his new found salvation and wants to tell others of his inner joys. This all comes about because some one took the gospel message to him and in so doing becomes his spiritual father.

"WHEN ABOMINABLE SIN MOVES IN"

I Corinthians 5:1-7

INTRODUCTION:

Shakespeare said, "One sin, I know, another doth provoke; murder's as near to lust as flame to smoke."

Sins are gregarious and one sin always breeds more. A bad tooth poisons the system and causes rheumatism. Contention over preachers creates an atmosphere in which every vile thing grows luxuriantly. Jealousy is followed by immorality, controversy, indifference, vanity, and gluttony. Paul advised that the incestuous person be expelled for his sake and for the sake of Christianity.

PROPOSITION: *When abominable sin moves into the congregation what should be done about it?*

I. IMMORAL, SELF-EVIDENT SIN IS NOT TO BE TOLERATED IN THE CHURCH.
   A. Sometimes professing church members bring in the vilest of sins even when the purest precepts are set forth in doctrine.
   B. Paul had founded this church in Corinth. I Cor. 9:1-2 + 4:15
      1. The sin in the Corinthian church was worse than that practiced among the heathen Gentiles. Vs. 1 The best fruit when it rots, seems to stink the worst. "Shall I come unto you with a rod?"
      2. This sin was held in reprobation; not countenanced among the heathen even of lowest moral standards.
   C. God had laws in the Old Testament dealing with this sin. Jesus gave a higher law than any of the Old Testament. Matt. 5:27-28
   D. We see that sin seeks to enter EVERYWHERE, and the more holy the surroundings the greater the mark of damnation. Black shows up on white!
      1. It would have imperiled the whole community. Vs. 6
      2. It would have reproduced and became very aggressive.
      3. It would have brought contempt upon the whole church. The church should never live in such a way so as to deserve contempt.

4. It would have killed the church's influence for good. If she is ritten within how can she fight sin outside?
5. It would have grieved Jesus. He died to redeem man from sin and to purify unto Himself a holy nation.
6. It would have invited the judgment of God upon them. God hates ALL sin and especially traitory.

II. WHEN ABOMINABLE SIN MOVES IN, THE CHURCH MUST DEAL WITH IT.

A. The offender must be out of the fellowship or communion. I Cor. 5:4-5
1. For lesser offenses, only a warning is given. Gal. 5:21 "I forewarn you, even as I did forewarn you."
2. It is good for the offender and for the church to publicly let it be known that the ungodly member has been disfellowshipped.
3. If the church treats sin lightly, then the offender will take it in the same spirit.
4. There is to be no partiality shown. The same treatment is to be given to the rich as well as to the poor.

B. The purpose of this disciplinary action is to reclaim the offender if it is at all possible. "that the spirit may be saved...."
1. Delivering him unto Satan was for the purpose of causing him to see the error of his ways and to repent. Apparently this immoral man did repent. II Cor. 2:5-11
2. The "flesh" refers here to the carnality that had caused the sin; it was to be destroyed by excommunication. Actually those who love the offending one, should desire that he be heavily afflicted, so he will repent. This will cause a reunion and a strengthening of the church as a whole.

III. WHEN ABOMINABLE SIN MOVES INTO THE CHURCH, IT SHOULD CAUSE THE MEMBERS TO REEXAMINE THEMSELVES IN RELATIONSHIP TO THE FALLEN ONE.

It certainly is a humiliating thing to the whole congregation.
1. There should be grief for the beloved one who had to be put out.
2. We should ask ourselves:
a. Did we care for him as we should have when he was with us?

b. Could we have checked the sin when it was small?
c. Did we pass up opportunities to save him before he went so far?
d. Did we look upon the sin as a light thing, not making it appear as it is, heinous and damning?

   This is one of the tragedies of our TV saturated society today; sin is seen so often we treat it lightly.

e. Was the offender led away and assisted downward by some church member who did not go quite that far in sin?
f. Could the general tone of the church (from the preacher on down), because of their laxity, have been the cause of his fall?

When great disgrace comes upon the church it should be a time for internal inspection, to make a careful inventory of the conditions to see what caused it, and to prevent further departures.

This illustration, "As an eagle stirreth up her nest," is one of the most beautiful and appropriate that could be conceived. It is taken from the habits of the eagle. When her young ones are well-fledged and would prefer to linger in downy ease, she disturbs the nest that they may be taught how to fly. Look at that eagle as she shoves the eaglet out of the nest and forces him to fly. That is what the church must do for those who will not grow, but who persist in remaining babies, undeveloped and a curse to the remaining members. The nest must be stirred and the evil put out that the cause of Christ be not blasphened or hindered.

"WHAT ASSOCIATION MAY THE CHRISTIAN HAVE WITH THE WICKED?"

I Corinthians 5:9-13

INTRODUCTION:

The Christians in any community that God names as His people are the ones who possess the Spirit of Christ and by their lives exemplify the character of Christ. These verses were directed to that true church, the body of Christ in Corinth. They were a professedly pure people so Paul urged them to purge out the old leaven, purify the place that had become impure, and then he explained to them how they can remain pure.

PROPOSITION: *How is the Christian to treat the wicked?*

I. HOW IS THE CHRISTIAN TO TREAT THE WICKED WHO ARE OUTSIDE THE FELLOWSHIP OF THE CHURCH? I Cor. 5:9-10

A. The Christian is not limited merely to the society of believers.

The Christian is to practice some "sanctified common sense."

a. If this sort of separation that some practice was compulsory, it would force all Christians to crawl into a hole, seek out a monastery or be hermits. "to go out of the world." Vs. 10

b. Our every day life causes us to rub shoulders with those who are lost and wicked, giving us an opportunity to witness to them. Titus 2:12 "...we should live soberly, righteously, and godly, in this present world."

c. Christ set the example as He mingled among men of all types.

d. The chief purpose of our living among men is to witness to them of our salvation and Jesus' saving power. We are, as Christians, actually ministers and missionaries.

e. We reach a class of people that the preacher can never reach, while we are living the gospel amidst the crooked and perverse.

B. We are never to lose sight of the perils of such associations.

1. Our first duty is to witness to them; our second duty is to be aware of the danger of being "taken in" by them!
2. A soldier goes armed when he enters the enemy's territory. Eph. 6:10-18
3. The Christian does not go alone among the world.
   a. He can go anywhere with Christ, if it is in the path of Christian duty.
   b. He must be in prayer, watching, and not in self-reliance.
4. The Christian must NEVER go further into the world than he knows is necessary for the ongoing of the kingdom of Christ.

II. HOW IS THE CHRISTIAN TO TREAT THE MAN WHO CLAIMS TO BE A FOLLOWER OF CHRIST, BUT IS LIVING A WICKED LIFE?

A. Here God gives a different rule for our conduct.

1. The outsider is a stranger to the grace of God and in need of Him; however the inside wicked man is identified with the church.
2. Those on the outside are already condemned by the judgment of God, Vs. 13 but the inside man is judged by every true Christian. He is an offending brother and we MUST sit in judgment on him. Vs. 12

B. There are degrees of sin in the church, and if the offender has gone too far in our judgment, based on the Word of God, he must be excommunicated until he repents.
1. We are to have NO fellowship with the wicked brother. Vs. 11
   a. This is to impress upon him what the church has decreed!
   b. This enforces church discipline and makes it more effective.
   c. Too many times in the past, the church as a body has disfellowshipped a wicked member, and individual members have continued to fellowship with him. By leaving him alone, the effect upon the offender is more meaningful.
2. Discipline is used as a means of restoring the brother who has wilfully erred, but if it is not enforced, the effect is lessened.
   If we do not disfellowship the wicked inside, it will appear to the man, and to the world as well, that we do not hate sin.
3. The church member should remember that it is often more dangerous to associate with the wicked insider than it is to associate with the lost man outside.

III. WHAT SINS DEMAND SEPARATION?

These are considered by the Holy Spirit inspired Apostle as the worst sins of the church. Vs. 11

1. Fornication...which is dealt with in full in the first verses.
2. Covetousness...those whose hearts are set on or have a strong desire for the things of this world.
3. Idolatry...those who claimed membership but continued to hobnob with the heathen image worshippers, perhaps attended their feasts and offered sacrifices (saved by Christ, and saved by Masonry at the same time).

4. Railing, revilers. Out of the fulness of the heart the mouth speaks. The mouth advertises the heart's condition.
5. Drunkenness...Deliberately partaking of drinks that produce idiotic actions and acts not indulged in even by the brute creation.
6. Extortion...those who are greedy and over-reach themselves in cheating others to make money.

With these inside sinners we are to have no fellowship. God does not forbid our praying for them; we should, but we are not to eat with them nor visit them as friends. Every Christian should do all he can to recover them. The first step toward their recovery is to have nothing to do with them until they are ashamed. Hell is the awful place where all the wicked are bound; they are cut off forever from the righteous. The wicked insider should be reminded of this as he rebels against the will of God.

A once earnest disciple lost his spirituality through the usual influence of worldly prosperity. He was disfellowshipped from the midst of believers but to no avail. God did not give him up, but took from him his wife by death, and then a beloved son; still he refused to turn. More misfortunes blighted his life but he refused to repent. A loathsome, incurable disease took hold of him and while he was helpless in his house the place caught fire. As he was carried from the burning building he shouted, "Blessed be God, I am cured at last." Shortly after that he died, but he died as one who had been brought back to God by DISCIPLINE.

"CHRISTIANS IN THE COURTS OF THE LAND"

I Corinthians 6:1-8

INTRODUCTION:

I stand amazed in the presence of this mighty book of God. It surpasses my own imagination how the Lord could reveal so many eternal truths and practical every-day problems and solve them in one book. Here the age old problem of settling disputes among brethren comes up. The church was being brought into ill repute by these unseemly litigations.

Considering the changes that have taken place in the "courts of the land," we need to ask ourselves just how far Paul's exhortation is to be applied today. In the courts of the Roman empire, often the judges could be bribed and the decision rendered unjust. Often times the litigants had to do obeisance to some false God before court opened. Refusal to comply often meant the recalcitrant was sure of injustice. Even in our day we have much injustice. Steal a loaf of bread and one is sentenced to jail for ten years; but steal a whole railroad system and one is awarded a place of honor on Wall Street.

Legal proceedings are allowable sometimes. Paul appealed to Caesar and escaped the judgment of the court. If, by allowing a criminal to escape just sentence, society is abused, we should go to court for the welfare of society.

PROPOSITION: *Court proceedings should be avoided by Christians because they injure the church.*

I. LITIGATION PUTS THE CHURCH IN A BAD LIGHT BEFORE THE COMMUNITY.
  A. Usually the litigants receive injury.
    1. A lawsuit is well represented by the owners holding the cow by separate ropes while the lawyers milk her; the principles furnish the money and the lawyers get rich.
    2. Morally and spiritually the ones going to law lose.
    3. The temptation to take advantage causes anger and ill feelings, if not absolute hatred between them.
    4. Court is a poor place to pray, "Forgive us our trespasses as we forgive those who have trespassed against us."
  B. In the minds of the public there is always injury to the church when its members sue each other. (It is a public spectacle.)
    1. It shows a lack in the church of men wise enough to decide.
    2. The world looks upon the fighting members as the true representation of the church; but in reality this is not true.
    3. It lowers men's estimate of the church and its message. Love, peace, forebearance and unity have failed in the very place where they are preached.
  C. Possibly, the worst thing about it is that it destroys confidence in the one institution that holds the power to save a lost world.

II. CHURCHES SHOULD STUDY TO SEE HOW LAW SUITS CAN BE AVOIDED.

A. Covetousness leads to lawsuits.
   1. If men wanted only what is rightfully and justly theirs, it would stop many going into court.
   2. Covetousness makes a man think he is dealing justly, when in reality, he is very selfish and unjust. I Cor. 5:9-11

B. The Christian should be willing to take less than he has coming to him, in order to avoid disgracing the church.
   1. Suffering wrongfully (I Peter 2:15-21) is a Christian trait.
   2. Self-sacrifice is the heart of Christianity. (Mark 8:34)

C. Two Christians, threatening each other with litigation, should consider that they are supposed to be brothers in the same family.
   1. They should be working for the Lord Jesus.
   2. They should ask themselves, "Will this litigation promote love of the brethren?"

D. When we choose up sides and oppose each other it often makes us poor judges of the other fellow. The "other" fellow becomes, in our minds, everything objectionable!

E. Presenting the problem to some wise Christian brother will often bring just settlement and save the good name of the church.
   1. Paul pleads for this proceedure, and punctuates his argument with sarcasm.

      He reminds them that people who claimed to be so superior should have men among them who are wise enough to take care of this problem. 6:2-5 cf. 4:8-10
   2. Paul reminds them that we are at some future date to be the judges of the world.

      Why not be making preparation now for this future great work by some practice in this field of judication where it is comparably simple? Vs. 3

We should remember in our judgments between ourselves and others, that one day we are to stand before the Lord in judgment. Then "with what judgment we have judged, we shall be judged." Let us be careful how we judge each other in the light of what the Lord has told us, relative to our own judgment. He will be the RIGHTEOUS judge and He will know everything we thought as well as the deeds we did. Only by His grace and mercy will any man be able to stand.

Each one of us is much like the man whose case was pending. "Will my case be called today?" he asked his lawyer. "Are you sure nothing has been left out? If the judge should pronounce against me, I am a ruined man."

His lawyer was a Christian man and he took this opportunity to inquire of him, "Are you a Christian, friend? Have you taken every precaution to see to it that your eternal judgment is going to be one that will please you? What if your case should be called before the eternal judge today? Would you be safe forever, or would you be a ruined man FOREVER?"

Some day the books will be opened and we will stand before the judge. We shall give an account for the deeds done in the body, whether unto life or death depends on our relationship to the Lord by His Son Jesus Christ.

"WE HAVE BEEN BOUGHT AND PAID FOR"

I Corinthians 6:12-20

INTRODUCTION:

Men of today could learn a valuable lesson from observing how the Apostle pursued sin and sought to destroy it among the followers of the Lord. Paul cries out in the plainest language possible, "Flee Fornication!" The shame is in having sin, not in rebuking it. Paul has listed specific sins that will shut the door of heaven to the church member. Vss. 9-10 These he exposes to the light of the spirit of God, and he ends this discourse section with, "Know ye not that your body is the temple of the Holy Spirit?" V19 He reminds them they were "bought with a price."

PROPOSITION: *What does Paul teach here?*

I. THE FACT STATED, "YE ARE BOUGHT WITH A PRICE," INDICATES THAT A TRANSACTION HAS TAKEN PLACE. Vs. 20
   A. This statement is being denied by the heretics who mask under the name of Neo-orthodox, or better, called plain Modernists.
      They speak of it as Mercantile religion; however, that is exactly what the Scriptures say, "Bought with a price."

B. This is a fact, not a misstatement! It is true that every person on earth is either redeemed by Christ, or unredeemed and damned.
   1. When we are redeemed from our sins, it is the greatest news to "roll from the press." John 3:15-17; I Tim. 2:6; Mark 10:45; Rom. 6:23; I Cor. 6:11; II Cor. 5:18
   2. This true message will become of more importance to you as the Judgment day draws near.
      It will never cease to be true, and it will never be surpassed in importance to the redeemed. "Able to save unto the uttermost—ALL...."
   3. This should make a tremendous impression on us, influencing our lives here, and giving impetus to our heavenly endeavors.

II. WHAT IS THE RESULT OF THIS TRANSACTION? "Ye are not your own." Vs. 19
   A. Nothing could be plainer. If you are bought you are not your own.
      1. Now you are sheep, provided for by the good Shepherd. Psalm 23
      2. You have taken aboard a Pilot; your ship is under His control.
         "Jesus Saviour pilot me, over life's tempestous sea...."
      3. Being the property of another, we have no right to injure our bodies or souls; He owns them. II Cor. 7:1
         a. Our time is His. We are not to waste it in idleness. We are not to waste it in amusements, no matter how harmless they may seem. Eph. 5:16
         b. We are to follow Him. We are not to follow our own prejudices, misguided affections, wills (that wander from the strait and narrow), or appetites of the flesh. Eph. 5:1
         c. We are to be slaves to God. Rom. 12:1-2
            (1) We no longer serve two masters; self and God, divided.
            (2) "This ONE thing I do." Phil. 3:13
         d. "...spirit and soul and body...." I Thess. 5:23

III. WHAT DOES GOD EXPECT OF US BECAUSE WE BELONG TO HIM?
   A. "Glorify God therefore, in your body."

1. Glorify God in a life of holiness. Titus 2:3; Rom. 6:22; I Thess. 3:13; II Cor. 7:1
2. Glorify God in temperance. Titus 2:2; II Peter 1:6
3. Glorify God in business. Heb. 6:12; Rom. 12:11
4. Glorify God in cheerfulness. Matt. 9:2; 14:27; John 16:13
5. Glorify God in patience. Lu. 21:19; Rom. 5:3; Col. 1:11

B. We should glorify God in whatever comes into our lives.
1. If we suffer long in the body before our demise;
2. If we have to work in difficult places;
3. If it is difficult to worship the Lord;
4. If those about us try to turn us aside;
5. If disobedience is on every hand;
6. We are still to glorify God in our bodies and Spirits, because they belong to Him.

William Robinson gives this illustration that well suits our text, "We are bought with a price."

"Why should so great a price be required? Is man worth the price? A man may be bought in some places of the world for the same price as an ox. So it was not man that had to be redeemed simply, but man in a certain relation. A man who has been a drunken, idle, worthless bum is worth nothing, but let that same man commit a crime for which he is to be hanged and then try to buy him from the authorities, try to redeem him and make him your servant. Let the richest man offer every cent he possesses for that worthless man, and his offer would be of no avail. Why? Because now there is not only the man to be considered, but the law he has broken and the government against which he has sinned. A very great price is required to redeem a man from the curse of the law of England; but Christ came to redeem all men from the curse of the Divine law, the broken law of Jehovah God."

"We are redeemed, but not with silver...."—Redeemed by the precious blood of the crucified Son of God. Precious price!! Oh, how we should love Him for buying us at such a price.

"WHAT DOES CHRISTIANITY TEACH ABOUT MARRIAGE?"

I Corinthians 7:1-6

INTRODUCTION:

The whole scope of the marriage relationship is not found in this scripture. In this particular instance Paul is answering some questions the Corinthians had asked relative to marriage in that period of stress. (7:26-28) To save them the double trouble of fleeing with a wife and children, in order to save their lives, Paul says it is better to remain single. However, he is not a mere theorist, so he takes into account human nature and says, "it is better to marry than to burn" (vs. 9), or to make one's self susceptible to the temptation of incontinency and fornication. It is better to get married and suffer the inconvenience of taking care of a wife and children for a while during this persecution, than to spend eternity in hell for the sin of fornication. (That is a long burn.)

Corinth was infamous for its moral corruption. Its society was corrupted by a religion that promoted immorality. The splendor of the city was only surpassed by its impurity. Idolatrous adultery was prevalent and openly made inviting and appealing to all, especially to the unmarried. This had inflicted the church, as seen in the fifth chapter where fornication was tolerated among its believers.

PROPOSITION: *What does Christianity teach concerning marriage and sex?*

I. LET US REMEMBER THAT GOD ORDAINED MARRIAGE. Gen. 1:27-28; Mal. 2:13-16; Matt. 19:3-9; Rom. 7:2-3
   A. God does not command that every person become married. Vss. 1,7,8
   B. He is not teaching that celibacy is better than marital union; God does not teach that. Heb. 13:4
      1. What would happen to the human race if celibacy was practiced?
         a. In about 70 years there would be no more people on the earth.
         b. A church without an audience; a school without a student.
      2. Sex is not to "run wild" promiscuously; neither is it to be forcefully or unnaturally restrained as in ascetic celibacy.
      3. God says "To avoid fornication, let every man have his own wife, and let every woman have her own husband." Vs. 2
         a. God knows us better than we like to admit at times.
         b. What a difference there would have been in history if this simple admonition had been heeded.

The last war serves to demonstrate what happens when a great army of single women and single men are let loose upon civilization... the disgrace of their actions has blackened the pages of our national history.

C. Jesus in Matthew 19:3-9 repeats and sanctions the original commandment relative to the lawfulness of marriage and its inviolability.

II. MARRIAGE PRODUCES SOME OF THE PUREST AND FINEST AFFECTIONS POSSIBLE TO PRODUCE IN HUMAN FORM. Eph. 5:22-33.

Successful marriage is built upon unselfishness. Vs. 4

1. Men and women are both by nature selfish, but love, the basis of true marriage, blots out selfishness.
2. The family revolves successfully around the sphere of self-denial, self-sacrifice, mutual helpfulness, and forebearance.

Most men who are bachelors, have remained so to escape the responsibilities and obligations of wedlock and to indulge in self-gratification.

III. GOD ORDAINED MARRIAGE TO PROTECT HIS PEOPLE FROM VICE AND TO HELP DEVELOP THE HIGHEST VIRTUE.

A. At first and through this passage Paul admits that because of the stress that was upon them it would be better for them to refrain from marriage. Vs. 26

B. Paul is very practical too, so he says; "nevertheless, to avoid fornication..."

1. In our sex-saturated-literature and Hollywood productions, the entire population is exposed to the temptation of ILLICIT SEX!
2. When two people marry they surrender their bodies to each other in genuine love. Each belongs to the other and the natural sex desire is thus provided for in God's economy.
3. It has been alleged that 80% of divorces start in the bedroom by the selfishness of one or both of the married parties.
   a. Paying attention to Vss. 3-5 would have avoided the divorce trouble.
   b. If there is to be abstinence from sex relations, it must be mutually agreed upon... "that Satan tempt you not for your incontinency."

IV. MARRIAGE, AS GIVEN BY THE LORD, IS MADE A TYPE OF THE CHURCH AND ITS RELATIONSHIP TO CHRIST. Eph. 5:25 + 32

Christ is presented as the bridegroom and the church as His bride.

1. The bridegroom that tarried in Matt. 25:5 represents Christ; the bride is the church adorned for her husband. Rev. 21:2
2. Christ loved the church, His bride, enough to die for her. Eph. 5:25
3. The church should love Him and be in subjection to Him. Eph. 5:26-27
4. Through this relationship, heaven is replenished.
5. In marriage, natural life begins, and in the church, spiritual life has its beginning.

In the offerings of animals at the nuptial sacrifices to Juno, the Goddess of wedlock, the gall was taken away and cast behind the altar. This was to signify that between the young couple there would be nothing of bitterness or discontent, but in their stead, sweetness and love should fill the whole space of their lives.

It should be so in marriage, and it should be so in the church of the Lord Jesus Christ. If every professed follower of Christ really loved, cherished and served Him as a bride should her husband, the world would see what God intended it should see when it looks at the church, His Son's Bride.

"THE MIXED MARRIAGE PROBLEM IN THE CHURCH"

I Corinthians 7:10-16

INTRODUCTION:

In this letter Paul deals with various problems that are encountered by Christians. The one discussed here is concerning the converted heathen and their relationship to their marriage partner. Jesus dealt with the believer's relationship to his wife or to her husband in the gospels. As the church spread over the world the problem naturally came up as to how a Christian should be related in marriage with the heathen and how they are supposed to regulate their lives in this peculiar relationship.

PROPOSITION: *This subject must be divided into two parts; in one, both are Christians and in the other, one is a Christian and the other is not.*

I. FIRST, THE CASE WHERE BOTH HUSBAND AND WIFE ARE CHRISTIANS.
   A. Revelation had already been given on this relationship. cf. Matt. 5:31-32; and Matt. 19:3-9
      1. With two believers, marriage is an unbreakable union for life. "til death do us part."
      2. If either of the believers breaks the wedlock contract, they are disobedient to God, and commit deliberate, and wilful sin.
      3. It is to be a perpetual relationship ordained of God for home and society. Gen. 2:24
   B. If for any reason the yoke becomes unbearable, the woman or man who separates from the other Christian, should not do so permanently.
      1. Possibly the man who mistreats his wife will treat her better if she is absent for a short time.
         a. No matter how severe it is, it must not be considered as breaking the marriage bond.
         b. The one who separates must either remain single for life or go back to husband or wife.
            (1) The marriage bond is not so lightly broken.
            (2) Christianity and Hollywood are quite different.
      2. Two married people living separated lives, is not what God intended. cf. I Cor. 7:2-5
         a. Whenever two Christians separate, it brings a scandal upon the church and disgraces the doctrine.
            (1) This should cause any wrangling couple to reconsider and be willing to suffer for the cause of Christ.
            (2) Adultery, committed by professing Christians, is not considered here; that sin breaks the marriage bond. Matt. 19:9
         b. Marriage demands the deepest and most profound thought before entering, for it is a contract that cannot be terminated aside from sin!

II. NOW THE CASE WHERE ONE OF A MARRIED COUPLE, LIVING IN HEATHENISM, IS CONVERTED TO CHRIST.
   A. No Christian should ever marry outside of Christ. I Cor. 7:39; II Cor. 6:14; 7:1

B. When one partner in a heathen marriage is converted, then this problem comes up, whether it is in America or in darkest Africa.
   1. There had been no revelation on mixed marriages before this.
   2. Jesus had only taught Jews, who were both believers.
   3. There was no mixed marriage problem.

C. He explains their conduct if the unbelieving partner chooses to live with the Christian. Vss. 12-13
   1. The Christian is to be true to the marriage vow and laws of Christianity relating to it.
      a. Marriage was ordained of God before Christianity came, and before anyone drifted into heathenism. The unbelieving partner is "set apart" by God's earlier law relating to marriage (sanctified). Gen. 2:23-24
      b. The Christian who remains true can possibly turn the unbeliever to the Lord. Vs. 16; I Peter 3:1-2
      c. The children are "clean" in that God ordained marriage, and in that relationship the unbeliever is obedient to God. (They are not bastards.)
         (1) God has always spoken out against illegitimate offsprings. Deut. 23:2
         (2) The marriage relationship sanctifies the child. Vs. 14 (Whether they be heathen or Christian)
   2. God demands that the Christian who is in the yoke with a nonchristian MUST remain; he or she can not break the marriage bond.

D. What is the proceedure if the unbeliever makes the separation?
   1. The Christian cannot force the unbeliever to live with him or her, as the case may be; it is useless to try.
   2. If the "unbeliever departs...a brother or a sister is not under bondage in such cases." (Specific instruction) Vs. 15
      a. The marriage contract is no longer binding.
      b. "God has called us in peace." If by departing, the unbeliever brings peace for the family, it is better that he go.
      c. Marriage is not slavery, forcing the one to follow the other; but it is a bond that can be broken by adultery or by the unbeliever departing.
      d. The Christian partner is to do everything that is possible and Christian to keep the home together,

but if the unbeliever WILL NOT abide with the believer, then the believer is not to be considered bound by the former marriage contract. "Not under bondage" means free!

e. The innocent party is not to be punished for the sin of his or her life. God is just and equitable.

This practical teaching should be given to the people of God instead of the Roman Catholic doctrine that marriage can NEVER be dissolved. (Unless you have money enough to buy off the high officials.)

Marriage is sacred, but it is not a slaves bond. It is mutual aggreement, not forced. It is NEVER to be broken by one who wears the name of Christ.

There is only one way to secure the permanency of marriage and that is to obey the Lord and "marry in the Lord" if you are a Christian. There is no permanency of marriage among heathen or among those who are married to wilfully rebellious heathen.

Marriage is a type of the Christian's relationship to Christ. Christ does not FORCE OR COMPEL the Christian to remain wedded to Him. The backslider, worlding, and apostate who deliberately leaves, chooses to depart from Christ. Christ does not consider Himself bound to him. Christ never breaks the bond of union, but the wilful deliberate sinner who leaves Christ, breaks the union and goes out to a damnation worse than he had at the first. II Peter 2:20-22.

So it is with the Christian. He never breaks the bond of marriage, "but if the unbelieving depart, let him depart, the brother or sister is not under bondage."

"CHRISTIAN RESPONSIBILITY TO OTHERS"

I Corinthians 8:4-13

INTRODUCTION:

Indifference to the welfare of others or offending the conscience of the weak is wrong. Eating meat that was offered in sacrifice might not harm a strong and enlightend Christian, but if the eating of it was going to hurt the weak brother, then the one who deliberately indulged in the meat offering, was not a very mature Christian. Christians should consider what the results of their conduct will be on those about them. Christian liberty is limited by the needs of others. Practicing self-denial and restraint arises from our duty and desire to glorify the Lord, by helping the weak to refrain from that which would harm them. The highest exercise of RIGHT is the surrender of that right for the welfare of others.

PROPOSITION: *This portion of scripture has three general teachings.*

I. THE FIRST TEACHING IS—OUR MORAL OBLIGATION AS CHRISTIANS DEPENDS UPON OUR RELATIONSHIP TO THE ONE GOD AND HIS ONLY BEGOTTEN SON. 8:4

A. In the midst of a whole society that was idolatrous and thought idols had power, this statement was like a bomb shell.

Paul taught the truth, that there is but ONE God and that idols are really nothing. They have no power, morally or spiritually.

B. Monotheism is peculiar to "Revealed Religion." No group of persons without Revelation ever became monotheistic.

Jesus spoke of God to His disciples as "Our Father."

a. By the new birth, we become His children, begotten of Him.

b. He is Spirit and "they that worship him must worship in spirit and in truth." John 4:24

c. He is the Creator of the universe and the sustainer of it. John 1:1 + Col. 1:16-17

d. He is the supreme end of our existence and the greatest object of the Christian's love.

e. He loved us enough to send His only begotten Son to be our propitiatory sacrifice.

He gave us a Mediator between Himself and man. (It was by grace.)

f. As Christians, we owe everything we have and are to Him.

Every blessing we receive comes from God through Christ.

g. This everlasting, omnipotent and omniscient God, God above all man-made-gods, has laid an obligation upon us which can never be changed or abrogated.

That obligation is our humble worship of Him.

II. THE SECOND TEACHING IS—THAT ACTIONS IN THEMSELVES MAY BE WRONG FOR ONE MAN AND NOT BE WRONG FOR ANOTHER.

A. The Christian, who has grown in Christ enough to realize that an idol is nothing, could eat the meat and do himself no harm.
   1. The meat was perfectly good; it was not spoiled.
   2. It had not been changed one bit by being offered to idols.
   3. Their consciences did not bother them, so there was nothing wrong in eating it.

B. The younger person in the faith, fresh out of idolatry, who still believed it wrong to eat meat sacrificed to idols, would sin in partaking of it (sin against his conscience). Vs. 7
   1. Whether the act was right or wrong depended upon the individual's conscience and his relationship to others.
      Anything that is against our own sense of right should be abstained from entirely; however conscience is a creature of education. Just because one's conscience does not condemn him, does not make a thing right in God's eyes.
   2. A man may be sincerely wrong; but if he is insincere, he is always wrong. "Let every man be persuaded in his own mind." What is relatively wrong for me, might not be wrong with you.

III. THE THIRD TEACHING HERE IS—THAT IT IS ALWAYS WRONG TO SIN AGAINST A WEAKER BROTHER'S CONSCIENCE, PUTTING A STUMBLING BLOCK IN HIS PATHWAY. Vss. 9-12

A. In respecting the conscience of a weak brother, we may be called upon to practice self-denial.
   1. Sometimes the mature Christian is not bothered at all by that which would cause a new Christian to stumble.
   2. Possibly Paul could have taken the hind-quarter of an animal sacrificed to Baal and eaten to his fill, without sinning at all.
      a. He was free in Christ, but he was not free to hurt his weaker brother.
      b. He willingly refrained from anything that would possibly offend the weaker brother.
   3. It is our duty to deny ourselves or forego some pleasures for the sake of the weaker brother. Rom. 14:21

B. Paul goes into detail about showing consideration to others.

By thoughtlessness or carelessness for others, we may wound them irrepairably.

a. They may stumble over us. Matt. 18:7
b. They may be tempted to do wrong because of us.
c. We may cause them to "perish." Vs. 11
d. Christ died for everyone, so surely we can practice some self-denial for the sake of the weaker ones.
e. When we refuse, we sin against Christ. Vs. 12
f. We should resolve with the Apostle Paul, "... I will eat no flesh..., Lest I make my brother to stumble." Vs. 13

When Agrippina, the mother of Nero, was told that if her son became Emperor he would murder her, she said, "I am content to perish if he may become Emperor." That should be our plea in regard to our weaker brother; our willingness to die, if needs be, that our weaker brother may reign some day with Christ. Christlikeness kills all selfishness. It is selfishness that makes us sin against our brethren.

"GREAT CHARACTERISTICS OF PAUL"

I Corinthians 9:1-21

INTRODUCTION:

The inner personality of an individual comes to light when we see him in a conflict. Previously Paul had admonished others to deny self; now in this chapter he illustrates his doctrine. He willingly curtails his Christian liberties to help others. Paul says he is free, and that he has all the rights possessed by the other Apostles and all Christians. Although some questioned his right to the Apostolic office, Paul proves by his teaching, power, and conduct that he was chosen by the Lord to this office.

PROPOSITION: *Out of this defense of his Apostleship, we see the great characteristics of the man, Paul.*

I. HE HAD FREEDOM FROM THE CEREMONIAL RESTRICTIONS BEING PRACTICED ABOUT HIM.

A. Paul was the greatest preacher that ever lived and occupied an office that only eleven other men could claim.

1. He was a reasoner, scholar, and orator both by natural talent and by years of training.
2. He was educated in the secular schools in Tarsus and in religion at the feet of Gamaliel, one of the greatest teachers.

B. In accord with what he had said about denying one's self because of a weaker brother, he affirmed that even though he was an Apostle he would not cause a brother to stumble by his knowledge and power.
1. He was "free," but he did not use his freedom as a cloak for wickedness.
2. No conventional customs bound him, as such.
   He was an Apostle and a maker of decrees and customs.
3. Paul could see the degradation of the leadership of his day, and the spiritual pauperism among the church leaders.
4. Paul did not care for the conventionalities of men or the ceremonies of religion being practiced. Would to God we could raise up men of convictions today to put to shame the hypocrisy and man-made forms in religion.

II. A GREAT HEART OF SERVICE WAS ANOTHER OUTSTANDING CHARACTERISTIC OF THE APOSTLE PAUL. WHO WAS WITH A GREATER SERVANT THAN HE? Cf. II Cor. 11.
He could appeal to the Corinthians—"are ye not my work in the Lord?"—because he had converted them and turned them from idols to the one true God.
1. Through his labors they had been freed from Satan and bound to the Lord of Glory (greatest work on earth).
2. The manner in which they had been converted should have been evidence enough to convince them of his Apostleship. I Cor. 1:4-7
   a. They had received all the gifts through Paul's hands.
   b. They were created anew in Christ Jesus.
3. Paul could remind them of the work he had accomplished, when they questioned his Apostleship.
   Compare him with any of the ones they recognized as Apostles.
4. A minister is a servant, and the way he establishes his place is in the work he turns out.

III. PAUL'S GREATNESS OF CHARACTER CAN BE SEEN IN HIS ABSTINENCE FROM CARNAL ENJOYMENTS OF LIFE.

A. He did not go "overboard" in eats or drinks. Vs. 4

B. While he had the right to have a wife, he forewent that right. Vs. 5

1. Possibly some questioned Paul's Apostleship because he was not married.

   He gives the qualifications for an elder as one who is married and has children in subjection. Some, possibly, got these two offices mixed up.

2. Paul affirms that he had the right to be married to a Christian, enjoy connubial privileges, banquet with the best, and form domestic relations; but he deliberately forewent all of these to serve Christ better. (He does not, however, enforce this upon others.)

IV. HIS INNER CHARACTER IS SEEN IN HIS FOREGOING THE JUST CLAIM HE HAD TO THEIR TEMPORAL SUPPORT, BECAUSE HE HAD MINISTERED TO THEIR HIGHER SPIRITUAL NEEDS. Vss. 6-16

A. He gives several reasons why they should have supported him.

1. First, he uses three illustrations from every day life to show his right to their support (soldier, farmer, and dairyman). Vs. 7

2. Next, he uses the principle of common equity by asking, "Which is higher, the material or the spiritual?"

   Paul had sown unto them spiritual things, so they should have given him the lesser, or material things, for his support. Vs. 11

3. He clinches his argument in vss. 13-14 as based upon vss. 9-10.

   a. God demanded that the owner feed the oxen that worked for him. Vs. 9

      He applies this to an Apostle as one working for them and needing to be fed.

   b. The priesthood of the Old Testament was supported by those whom they served. Vs. 13 Lev. 27:26-33; Lev. 6:16-26

   c. The 14th verse specifies the same amount was to be given to those who preach the gospel. Luke 10:7

      He says the "Lord ordained" this merely to give them a living, not to make them rich.

B. Paul did not use this RIGHT, because he did not want to hinder the progress of the gospel. Vs. 12 It takes a great man to deny himself these rights, to promote the cause of Christ. He had denied himself feasts, married life, common business pleasures and greatest of all, his just support. The purpose of his self-denial was to show them that he practiced what he preached, and also the kingdom of Christ should not be hindered.

Paul's self-control and self-denial were not of his own nature, for he had been a proud man of high position and possibly of some means. When Christ came into his life, the change was made. Saul, the persecutor and proud Pharisee died, and Christ came to live within him. Our only hope for victory in this world, is for Christ to reign from within us. There must be surrender, complete surrender. God must become Lord of ALL or He is not Lord at all. Won't you yield to Jesus today, friend, and hand in your poor sinful life for His rich victorious one?

"PREACHING BECAUSE I MUST"

I Corinthians 9:16-17

INTRODUCTION:

The man, who preaches God's message faithfully, is one who has made a choice after weighing the various aspects of the "calling." He knows that preaching is not going to be easy; it never has been. He knows that the fruits of his labor will often be disheartening for long periods. He knows, too, that the joys of a life that is dedicated to God, far surpass the trials he must face. (II Cor. 4:17) The true preacher of the word is impelled to preach because the command of the Lord has reached his heart and he knows that he is fitted for the task. He does not listen to anyone else, but only to God in this call. Paul wrote, "Woe unto me if I preach not the Gospel!" (I Cor. 9:16) He knew that his disobedience to the call would be offensive to God and the blood of the lost would be upon his hands.

In this sermon, I want to examine with you the inner workings of the great preacher, Paul. We can always profit by studying the life of any one who has succeeded in the profession we are planning to follow. Paul is probably the best model we could find, and we want to see how he felt about preaching by impulse.

I. PAUL REALIZED THE HONOR OF THE PREACHER'S OFFICE.

A. It is the main office in the only heavenly institution on the earth that has eternity written on it. Matt. 16:18

1. Men are divinely called to this work by God, and they consecrate themselves to it.
   a. No one forces them into this vocation.
   b. They are supposed to live by this work. Vs. 14
2. Paul denies any "self-glorying" so we surmise there could easily be self-exaltation. Vs. 16
   a. Men have given social elevation to the clergy; referring to them as "The" Priests; giving them fine salaries and even finer robes.
   b. This has degraded the preachers calling by giving it wrong motives.
3. This calling brings man into a closer companionship with God. The invisible things of the other world become real to him.
4. As a preacher, he is in a purely spiritual relationship with his fellowmen, which is not true of other professions.
   a. Other relationships may be superficial, but the preacher deals with the eternal part of man, his soul.
   b. He "knows no man after the flesh."
   c. He watches for men's souls as one "who must give account."
5. He walks in the shadow of an endless eternity with God.
   a. All earthly businesses end at the grave, or perhaps before that time.
   b. The preacher is dealing with spiritual and moral influences that reach out into eternity.
      (1) He is the infinite developer of mankind.
      (2) He sows the seed for an eternal crop.

II. PAUL FELT A SENSE OF HIS OWN UNWORTHINESS TO FILL THIS OFFICE.

A. It made Paul a humble man to serve the Lord. Acts 20:19

1. The humble are to be exalted. Luke 14:11
2. Paul said, "Who is sufficient for these things?" II Cor. 2:16
3. Paul knew he was called of God and spiritually qualified; therefore he went about preaching the word and defending his Apostleship.

B. Constantly, Paul realized it was not he, personally, but that he was a chosen instrument in the hand of God. I Cor. 3:5-7
   1. He proclaimed the mercy of God to sinners, but he realized he also stood in desperate need of that mercy. I Tim. 1:15-16
   2. Paul's preaching against sin constantly warned him, more than anyone else, of his inner heart condition and need to walk circumspectly.
   3. Paul knew that preachers are tempted in subtle ways above all other people and it kept him humble.
   4. His words in vs. 27 seem to have hung over the head of this greatest of all preachers, keeping him "urgent in season and out of season."

III. PAUL REALIZED THAT PREACHING WAS SERIOUS BUSINESS.

A. A very important stewardship had been entrusted to Paul and he must be faithful.
   1. It is God's only method for making His salvation known.
   2. Necessity was laid upon Paul from an inward appeal. He was conscious of his eternal loss if he did not function faithfully.

B. Paul could do anything he wanted to do; but he WANTED to preach this message of salvation through the crucified Christ, above everything else on earth. This was the impulse of his heart.
   1. Paul had been set apart for this work from his mother's womb. Gal. 1:15; Rom. 1:1; and Acts 9:15
   2. Paul expresses it in Gal. 2:20.
      a. He had died and now the will of God was his will. II Cor. 5:14
      b. His love for Christ made him His slave, a bond servant of love.
      c. He joyously served Christ.

C. Paul realized the harvest was great and that it was ripe. Under the divine commission of the Heavenly King, he went forth to do His will with a sincere heart.

I pray God will raise up laborers that will have the same moving spirit as the Apostle Paul.

On Prince Street in Edinburgh, among the memorials of soldiers, poets, and scholars, one likes to see the monument to the great Scottish preacher, Thomas Guthrie. Taking refuge

under his arm is one of the waifs of the street; the Arabs for whom Guthrie founded the "Ragged Schools" through which he sought to save them for Christ. The poem he loved is the key of a great ministry. "I live for those who love me,
For those who know me true,
For the heaven that smiles above me,
And awaits my Spirit too;
For the cause that lacks assistance,
For the wrong that needs resistance,
For the future in the distance,
AND THE GOOD THAT I CAN DO."

Paul looked forward to receiving the crown. II Tim. 4:8

"THE CHRISTIAN LIFE REFERRED TO AS A RACE"

I Corinthians 9:24-25

INTRODUCTION:

Referring to the Christian life as a "race" would be very acceptable and very appealing to the people of Corinth, for it was here that great interest was aroused concerning the Isthmian games. Gambling on them became a national disgrace as gangsters moved in to take over the betting and "fixing" of the races. Every young man of athletic ability coveted the prizes that were given at these contests. People came from all over the Roman Empire to compete. It was a strategic move when the Holy Spirit moved Paul to appeal to the Christians to suffer for the cause of Christ as the athletes did for the prizes they won.

PROPOSITION: *How is the Christian life or "race" like the races of Paul's day?*

I. AS THE RUNNERS HAD A PLACE TO RUN, SO CHRISTIANS HAVE A PLACE TO RUN.

They ran in a great marble stadium; however Christians run every day in the world arena.

1. They are entered in the race of faith, obedience, love and patience, devotion to God and humble service to man.
2. Instead of running before a few thousand people in an arena, Christians are watched by all the world, both saints and sinners, while the hosts of heaven look down upon the course. Hebrews 12

II. AS THE RUNNERS WERE WATCHED BY INTERESTED ROOTERS FROM HOME AND ABROAD, SO CHRISTIANS ARE BEING WATCHED.

A. As they are being watched, Christians either bring a desire within the hearts of the onlookers to run the race with them or they cause them to look with disdain upon the race being run.

B. The great politicians, statesmen, merchants and salesmen were there in Corinth to watch the men who ran.

Christians run before the "great cloud of witnesses;" the Lord and all the saints. (Sometimes, I am afraid they are justified in being anxious as to the outcome.)

III. WHO PARTICIPATES IN THIS RACE?

A. It is not a race of preachers, elders, deacons and teachers alone; it is for every "born again" spiritual runner.

1. They run either to the glory of God or to His shame.
2. They wear His colors.

B. There is no respect of persons in this race; each man must answer for himself at the end. Rom. 14:12

IV. JUST AS THE RUNNERS HAD RULES IN THE RACES, SO CHRISTIANS HAVE RULES.

There is a training time and place for both.

1. Runners had to practice severe discipline, and obey the trainer.
2. They had to give up many things others enjoyed to get in shape.
   a. Certain foods they must eat.
   b. Weights worn on feet while training.
   c. Certain foods they must not eat.
   d. Regular hours; enduring fatigue and hardships.
3. Christians have much training to do.
   a. Learn the Word of God.
   b. Sacrifice time to equip themselves for the race.
   c. They must know the rules, so they can strive legally.
   d. They must learn to obey divine commands and live under the rules of God.

V. WHAT EFFORT IS DEMANDED IN THE RACE?

Just as the runners had to put forth very strenuous effort to finish the course, so it is with the Christians in God's race.

1. They must be willing to put everything they have into the race.
2. They cannot be lazy, nor become weary and lag.
3. They are to imitate those victorious runners, not the ones who "fizzled out."
4. Paul says, "SO RUN!"
5. They must be diligent, watching to gain an advantage, and enduring with full speed unto the end of the course.

VI. JUST AS THE RUNNERS RAN FOR A PRIZE, SO CHRISTIANS RUN TO GAIN THE INCORRUPTIBLE CROWN. 9:24-27.

A. The crown the Isthmian runners received was a chaplet of pine leaves.
   1. It was very short-lived.
   2. It was coveted to such an extent, that some men actually died from overexertion in order to win it.

B. Christians have an eternal crown that "Fadeth not away."
   1. It is the crown of life. II Tim. 4:8
   2. It is given by the Lord of heaven and earth to those who know why and how they have run the course He has set.
   3. We should extend ourselves every hour of the day to attain the incorruptible crown of eternal glory.

No man can win a race unless he enters one, and one cannot finish a race if he has not begun it. If you have not become a Christian, now is the time to begin the race. When one accepts Christ, he begins the Christian race. For the rest of his life he must run the race effectively if he expects to receive a crown at the finish. Now is the time to enroll, and train, and run.

In this race it is not the sprinter who wins, but it is the man who steadily lives for God day by day. It is much like the settlers that came across the great plains. They did not stop to measure how far they had come or how far they must go, but rather, day by day they marched on. They camped at night, fed the stock, ate, and rested just long enough to get up early and get into the race for the next day. At the end of their journey was the beautiful and fertile West Coast country. We live every day, and perhaps life does not seem like much at the end of each day, but after the years have passed before us, there comes a time to end the race of life. It is in the courts of heaven where we finish the race and receive the crown. II Tim. 4:7-8

Start today—Now!

"CHRIST THAT ROCK"

I Corinthians 10:4

INTRODUCTION:

Christ, who is so precious to our souls, is described by many and varied nomenclatures of distinction. He is referred to as "The Sun of righteousness," "bright and morning star," "Manna," "Living Bread," "The light of the world," "The city of refuge," "The Living Stone," "The foundation," and "the Rock."

PROPOSITION: *The Rock referred to in our text is a type of Christ.*

I. LIKE THE ROCK, CHRIST IS FIRM AND STABLE.
   A. Rock makes the most firm foundation.
      It is an emblem of strength. cf. Matt. 7:24; Luke 6:47
         Storms, violent winds, and flooding torrents do not move rock.
   B. Christ is a firm foundation. Matt. 16:18; Isa. 28:16
      Satan's power and fury, the influence of error, and the scoffs of the unbeliever can be successfully defied when we abide in Christ. Rom. 8:31-39

II. LIKE THE ROCK, CHRIST IS DISTINGUISHED BY ELEVATION.
   The base of the rock is deeply seated in the earth, but its top usually surpasses the surrounding topography.
   1. Christ stands out above all others in His dignity and exaltation. Phil. 2:6-11
   2. He is higher than the angels; He is King of Kings; He is Lord of Lords; He rules the Universe, visible and invisible. Col. 1:17-18

III. LIKE THE PEOPLE WHO DWELT IN ANCIENT ROCKS, SO WE DWELL IN CHRIST.
   They hewed houses in the rocks. Isa. 22:16;
      Christ, God manifest, is the Christian's dwelling place. Psa. 90:1
      a. Like the dove of old, we dwell in the cleft of the rock. Jere. 48:28; 91:9; I John 4:16

b. We are baptized INTO Christ and then we are to grow-up in Him. Gal. 3:27; Col. 3:1-4

IV. LIKE THE ROCKS OF OLD, CHRIST PROVIDES OUR REFUGE AND DEFENSE.

A. The fleeing enemy often found refuge among the rocks and in caves. I Sam. 13:6

This gave them security and safety from the flying arrows or horse-drawn chariots.

B. God in Christ is the refuge of His people when the enemy comes in like a flood. Heb. 6:18-20

1. The Old Testament Psalmist triumphed in Psa. 46:1-7.
2. Christ is the insurmountable defense for His church. Isa. 4:5-6
3. He will never desert us. Psa. 27:1-5; 143:7-9

V. LIKE THE ROCKS IN ISRAEL, CHRIST GIVES FORTH HONEY, OR SWEETNESS. Psa. 81:16; Deut. 32:13

To the Christian, all sweet peace and precious comfort come from our Rock, Christ Jesus. II Peter 1:4.

His promises are sweeter than the honeycomb. Psa. 19:10

VI. LIKE ROCKS THAT YIELD THE PUREST WATER, SO THE PURITY OF CHRIST YIELDS THAT WHICH ASSUAGES OUR THIRST.

A. Moses was commanded to smite the rock: (Ex. 17:5-6). Christ, our Rock, was smitten by Divine Justice for us.

1. He was "smitten of God, and afflicted, but he was wounded for our transgressions...." Isa. 53:4-5

From Him flows the divine stream of pardon and justification.

(1) God predicted this in Isa. 41:17-29.
(2) Jesus said, "If any man thirst, let him come unto me, and drink." John 7:37-39.
(3) A Divine promise for us. Isa. 55:1

2. As an abundance of water came forth when Moses smote the rock, so in Christ we have abundant pardon. Rev. 22:17
3. The God who supplied the water at Rephidim also provided the Israelites with water for the whole trip through the desert; so in Christ we have the water of life, for ALL our lives.

VII. LIKE ROCKS THAT SHELTER THE WAYFARER, SO CHRIST IS OUR "SHADOW OF A GREAT ROCK IN A WEARY LAND." Isa. 4:6; 25:4; 32:2

A. To God's people the Apostle could say, "If any man sin, we have an advocate.... Christ the righteous."
  1. In Christ we find shelter from the accuser.
    a. Our own consciences are cleared from the condemnation of the law and they are put to silence.
  2. In Christ we find shelter from the wrath of God, a God-provided shelter.

VIII. LIKE THE ROCKS ARE DURABLE, SO CHRIST IS EVERLASTING.

A. Rocks are difficult to move; they are lasting.
  1. It takes much wear over a long period to make any mark on them.
  2. Rocks remain from one generation to another for thousands of years.
    a. Jesus has more durability than the rocks of the mountains.
      (1) He is "The Rock of Ages."
      (2) He is "Deity," "The same yesterday, today, and forever."
      (3) The richness of His Grace will never wear through, nor become shattered. Heb. 1:10

IX. LIKE HIGH ROCKS IN A DESERT, CHRIST, BY HIS HIGH POSITION, GIVES US A GOOD LOOK AT THE DISTANT COUNTRY, OUR "PROMISED LAND."

A. The Israelite people as described by Balaam from a rock, were innumerable. Numbers 23:9

B. Moses on Mt. Pisgah could look into the land of promise; so the child of God, on Christ Jesus, hidden in Christ, can look with unfailing eye into the "better land," our heaven.

We, in Christ, can behold "The king in His beauty," from afar!

"As all waters meet in the sea, and as all the lights meet in the sun, so all the perfections and the excellencies of all the saints and angels meet in Christ! Christ has not only the holiness of angels, the loveliness of saints, and the treasures of heaven, but also the fullness of the Godhead—the riches of the Deity, are all in HIM." For it has pleased the Father that in Him should all fullness of the Godhead dwell; fullness of grace, fullness of knowledge, fullness of love, and fullness of glory. He is our ROCK, and as Jehovah led Israel, so Christ leads us in all of life and eternity.

"TWO CHARACTERISTICS OF ISRAEL"

I Corinthians 10:1-12

INTRODUCTION:

Israel's characteristics are clearly portrayed in this text. They are taken from the lives of a people who had a rich and long history. They were recorded for our instruction and for the profit of all succeeding generations. God, through inspired men, recorded the things that were best for us.

PROPOSITION: *The prominence of these characteristics.*

I. ISRAEL WAS A PEOPLE TO WHOM GOD GAVE GREAT PRIVILEGES.
   A. Like God's people in every generation, they enjoyed many privileges that were denied to others.
      1. All the people of Israel "were under the cloud." Vs. 1
         a. In this manner God protected them.
            (1) His protection is superior to all other protectors.
            (2) He gave them protection from the sun by the cloud and they had God's "street lights" at night. Ex. 13:21
         b. Others paid "protection money" and bought allies at a high price, while Israel had GOD to protect them. Who can be more safe than those whom God protects? Vss. 12-13
         c. Israel was looked upon as weak; but with God, she was stronger than the strongest, even Egypt could not stand against her!
      2. All the people of Israel "passed through the sea." Vs. 1
         a. They had been delivered from a menacing, fearful danger by yielding to God.
            (1) They walked into the sea and out, protected by God.
            (2) God opened the way for them.

(3) It looked impossible to Israel, but with God all things are possible.

3. They "were all baptized into Moses." Vs. 2
   a. They accepted Moses as their leader, became his disciples, and swore to follow him, as he led them for God. Ex. 19:7-8
   b. They followed a man whom God spoke through and to whom God spoke "face to face."

      We are baptized into a far greater name, for we are "baptized into Christ," (Gal. 3:27) by "water and the Spirit." John 3:5.
4. They "did all eat the same spiritual meat;" V.3
   a. God sent them bread from heaven fit for angels, and supplemented it with quail. (quail on toast) Ex. 16:13-15
   b. This should have been "bread" for their spirits as well, as they realized their helplessness in the desert.
5. They "did all drink the same spiritual drink:" even in that desert. Vs. 4
   a. The rock was Christ.

      He supplied their needs, just as He supplies our Spiritual food. Phil. 4:13
   b. The prophesied Messiah was in their midst; although unseen. He was their provider through miracles, and their ruler through Moses.
   c. He did not fail them; even though they were always in the wilderness.

II. THE SECOND CHARACTERISTIC OF ISRAEL WAS THEIR CONSTANT TRANSGRESSION.

A. They were not content with God's blessings, but lusted after evil things about them.

1. Their appetites were not longing for "heavenly food," (Ex. 16:15) but instead they longed for "slave food," onions, garlic and fish. Num. 11:5
   a. They seemed to forget that they had been SLAVES while they ate that food.
   b. Often those who have been delivered from sin, are tempted to go back and enjoy their former lusts. (Ex. 16:3)

      All of the epistles were written to help us not to return to our former life of sin and dissipation.

2. Without realizing it, they became idolaters. (golden calf) Ex. chp. 32
   a. They broke God's first commandment to them, possibly intending to make it only a symbol of Deity.
   b. They went down fast, ending in the awful evils associated with idolatry. Ex. 32:25-28
   c. They played with fire and were burned.
      Sin gradually declines the spiritual status of those who trifle with it.
   d. They forgot who had delivered them, fed them and given them drink.
      With full bellies they turned from their blessed God to their own curse. Jere. 5:7-8; 13:25-27
   e. In the same mountain where they had said, "All thou sayest we will do" they sinned publicly.
      The Christians in Corinth were coming awfully near to idolatry when they desired to eat the meat sacrificed to idols. Vss. 18-22
      (a) They did not see their danger!
      (b) We laugh at danger and the devil laughs at us!

The Israelites had many privileges, yet they sinned greatly and received great punishment. They were afflicted by the sword, Ex. 22:24; the plague, Nu. 16:46-50; and by the serpents, Nu. 21:6. Surely "God is not mocked" for they reaped what they sowed.

We, in this "land of the free and the home of the brave," who have had the gospel freely preached to us, are certainly privileged as a people; yet we have drifted and deliberately sinned against God and have become friends with "the enemy of Christianity," Roman Catholicism. Our privileges have made us all the more responsible, and our judgment will be all the heavier unless we turn to the Lord in genuine repentance.

The Lord willingly extended salvation to the very people who had crucified His Son. Peter said to those enlightened and privileged people, "Repent ye and turn again, that your sins may be blotted out and so there may come seasons of refreshing from the presence of the Lord." It all depended upon their turning. So our salvation depends upon our turning to the Lord. "Why will ye die?"

"THE CHRISTIAN AND TEMPTATION"

I Corinthians 10:13

INTRODUCTION:

Although this letter is filled with warnings, there is also this heart warming encouragement given to those who were being tested, those who were too "cock-sure" of themselves. They were warned to beware lest they fall. Paul assured them that when temptation does come the Lord will not desert them to the enemy, but will stand by them to strengthen them for victory. This should be a source of encouragement to all those who aspire to high development in their Spiritual lives.

PROPOSITION: *What God has said about temptation to the Christian.*

I. BE SURE THAT TEMPTATION WILL COME TO YOU; IT IS UNIVERSAL.
  A. To avoid temptation in this old world is impossible.
    1. Temptation came to all of the Apostles, including the writer of this epistle.
    2. Jesus was tempted in the wilderness. Matt. 4:1-11
       He was tempted in all points just as we are. Heb. 4:15
    3. Temptation should not be regarded as a sign that we are in disfavor with God.
       Abraham was tempted. Gen. chp. 12
  B. Many who have met temptation and overcome it have lived to "count it all joy." James 1:2

II. THERE IS A VAST DIFFERENCE BETWEEN TEMPTATION AND SIN; TEMPTATION IS NOT SIN!
  A. Sensitive souls are often more aware of temptation than the "dead" sinner.
    1. The devil goes after "live ducks who are trying to get away," and not after those who are already "dead ducks!"
    2. When men hunt for bear they use "bear guns," likewise the devil uses the biggest guns he has on the Christians.

3. The devil sees no need of shooting at dead soldiers, but at those who might do him harm, he sends strong temptations.

B. The Christian who resists temptation lives to be tempted again.

1. The devil will not leave you alone as long as you belong to Christ. II Tim. 3:12
2. Until a person consents to the devil's temptation and succumbs, it is not sin.
   a. Where there is no consent, there is no sin.
   b. The sinless Christ was tempted for forty days. Luke 4:1-13

III. JUST BECAUSE WE ARE TEMPTED, WE ARE NOT COMPELLED TO COMMIT SIN!

A. No matter how enticing the devil makes sin appear, he can not compel us to accept his bait.

1. The only approach the devil can make is temptation, trying us; but he can not force us to accept his design.
2. Sin must be entered into by consent.
   a. If we are compelled to sin, then it is not sin. The maiden who was "raped by force" was not considered a sinner, nor was she punished as such. II Sam. 13:12-14.

B. Satan's strongest approach is inducement.

1. He said to Jesus, "Cast thyself down"; but notice he could not compel Him to obey!
2. Because sin must be entered into voluntarily, we are accountable for our yielding.

   WE are the guilty one, no one else.

IV. HOW GOD HELPS US WHEN WE ARE TEMPTED.

A. God is faithful and when we are being tempted, He will come to our rescue.

1. If we will trust Him, He will not let us be tempted above our abilities.
2. God never tempts us for an evil purpose.

   His help is always forth-coming to those who ask for it. I Thess. 5:24
3. He does not shield us from temptation, but He provides a way of escape sufficient for us.
   a. He did it for Job and cleared his name.
   b. He helped Paul bear his infirmities. II Corinthians 12:8-9
   c. God helps us to meet, bear, and defeat temptations.

4. There is only one way to defeat Satan and that is to look to God, our High tower, buckler and sword, that we may stand against the "wiles of the Devil." Eph. 6:11
   a. No man is strong enough to defeat the devil ALONE; but those who are in alliance with God, cannot be taken in by the devil.
   b. Only as we are in covenant relationship with God through the Lord Jesus Christ, can we overcome the devil and defeat him to the glory of God, and to the salvation of our souls.

William Lynford was asked, a short time before he passed away, the reason for the hope he had in the future. Stretching forth his hand he said, "Here is the grave, the wrath of God, and the devouring flame. It is the just punishment for sin to all men. It is on one side and I am on the other, poor weak sinner that I am. This is my comfort, the covenant of Grace established upon so many sure promises of God. It is able to save any sinner who comes to God by way of the cross. There is an "act of oblivion" past in heaven; "I will forgive their iniquities, and their sins will I remember no more." Jesus saved me from my past sin, came into my life to give me strength to overcome Satan, and promises to take me safely over Jordan. THAT IS MY HOPE."

Oh, sinner, I would to God you would hear that same blessed message of salvation and hope; NOW, before the gate of His mercy is closed forever.

"THE CHRISTIAN'S CANON OF CONDUCT"

I Corinthians 10:31-33

INTRODUCTION:

The word "canon" means that which has been measured and found adequate. God gave this canon, so we are assured that it is both appropriate and sufficient for all of life's problems. No one can overestimate the importance of rules. They limit our lives like the banks of a river, and they give depth to our motives.

PROPOSITION: *Notice the wide field this law covers for us, and in the mind of God.*

I. WHAT IT IS AND WHAT IT DOES.
  A. It is a rule that seeks to glorify God and please good men.
    1. Men have made and are making endless rules, but this one alone is without a flaw.
       It comes close to restating Matt. 22:37-39
    2. The rule of some people is to magnify self, while others live to please ALL men, both good and wicked.
      a. This makes us many friends, but will not please God.
      b. God is our axis, center and core; our attitude toward Him should be our first concern, then our fellowmen.
    3. This rule is reasonable because God created us, sustains us, and we must answer to Him for our every deed.
    4. This rule brings the highest benefits.
      a. God stated it because He wants to bless us because we obey.
      b. To disobey it, we bring frustration upon ourself, dishonor to God, and injury to our neighbor.
      c. We bring life to others by its product or we bring death by breaking it.
    5. By observing this rule, we experience the greatest joy known to man, not merely a "kick" out of living.
      a. There is no artificial stimuli needed.
      b. This heavenly rule brings heavenly joy!

II. HOW APPLICABLE IS THIS GREAT RULE OF LIFE?
  A. God's greatest rule for man applies to everything in life.
    1. From the Source of life, comes the rule of life for every phase of life.
      a. It applies to small and great events in life.
      b. It applies to secular and sacred events as well.
      c. By it, they become the same to glorify God.
  B. This rule makes everything we do interesting and helpful.
    1. Paul emphasized the most repeated activities of life, eating and drinking. Vs. 31
      a. By observing this rule, we will overcome the sins of gluttony and laziness.
         We will eat and drink so we can be the most efficient servant of God.
      b. A mere show of religion on Sunday is not Christianity.
         That is hypocrisy, which is easily detected by the world.

C. This rule makes our religion unbroken, steadfast and fruitful.
   1. True religion is always continuous and functional.
      a. This one thought, uppermost in our minds, would change our outlook on life completely!
         (1) Selfishness would die; it is the center of all sin.
         (2) Many worldly activities would cease, because we could not do them to the glory of God or to the benefit of others.

D. This rule is the source and fruit of the truly, beautiful Christian life.

III. WHAT IS UNFOLDED OR BROUGHT TO LIGHT BY THIS RULE?

A. It can only come after the natural, carnal man has been converted.
   1. Only Christ reigning within makes men behave in this manner.
   2. Until we are converted we fight against God and His laws.
   3. God has appointed the way by which we can be changed; no other way is acceptable to Him.
      We do not prescribe our own medicine; nor invent our own panacea.
   4. We must be converted to the Lord Jesus, by the power of God, in order to serve God acceptably. Col. 3:17; John 3:3-5

B. True service begins with a right relationship to God.
   1. Any man who truly wishes to serve God, will behave himself properly toward his fellowman.
      It is true religion that fits EVERY act of life.
   2. Even in self-improvement, if it is done to glorify God, it is proper. II Tim. 2:15 "God's workman."
   3. In our relationship to others, we must not forget our relationship to God.
      Matt. 22:37-39 makes it evident that the two laws are inseparable.
   4. This rule will make us consider the conscience of the weaker brother, (vs. 28) not merely our own self-willed conscience.
      a. By this rule, we will seek to build him up in the most holy faith, and never tear him down thoughtlessly.

b. The salvation of OTHERS grows out of this rule, not out of some carnal contest. V33.
c. Denying our own selfish wishes grows out of the new life from God and produces, naturally, this Christian canon of conduct.

I have just returned from the funeral of a man who demonstrated this text. He was anything but a Christian when first we met. Through listening to "the Gospel, the power of God unto salvation" he became an obedient believer. He was genuinely converted. His stingy, selfish heart was changed to an unselfish central station for dispensing God's blessings on others. His ungodly temper and fast fists became famous for Godliness and patience. His old enemies noticed the change in his life, and many of his associates were won to Christ. Glorifying God and helping others became the rule of his life and it can become yours today. Christ has opened the way. Will you not walk in it? Begin right now!

"THE HEAD OF EVERY MAN IS CHRIST"

I Corinthians 11:3

INTRODUCTION:

While the specific instance to which Paul referred to here has gone into the almost forgotten annals of history, the principle propounded in connection with it holds good for all time. Long hair and a veil are not becoming to men; they are woman's adornments. Man holds his own peculiar place. He was not made for woman, but woman for man. Women who profess Christ should not dress gaudily, nor make a display of themselves in the public assembly, but they should "learn in quietness." This principle holds for all time.

PROPOSITION: *The authority or "headship" of Christ for both men and women has certain distinct phases.*

I. IN CHRIST, WE SEE PERFECT HUMAN NATURE.
  A. He was the perfect manifestation of manhood, "the fairest of ten thousand."
    1. Pilate spoke of Him as "The Man."
    2. He is the head of a "New Creation."

a. He was untainted from the fallen human stock.
b. He was incarnated Deity.
He came from heaven. I Cor. 15:47
3. As perfect as the first "Adam," fresh from the hand of God, Jesus retained His purity.
a. Adam lost his sinless, symmetrical perfection by succumbing to the delusion of sin, and became the father of a sinful degenerate humanity.
b. It will never be that pure again.
4. God gave the promise of a coming "Seed" that would crush the serpent's head.
a. Gal. 4:4 says, "In the fulness of time, God sent forth his son...."
b. He was true, perfect manhood, yet mysteriously linked with Deity. "The first born among many brethren."
5. His mission was to "Lead many sons to glory."
B. To see the possibilities God has for us, what we can and ought to be, we can see them only in Christ.
1. Artists, in every age and among all people, have pictured Christ in various degrees of majesty and tenderness.
a. Some are exaggerations, for no artist can ever portray Him in all His fulness.
2. He is to be admired, adored, and worshiped, forever the example of a perfect man.

II. WE SEE IN CHRIST THE SOURCE OF ETERNAL LIFE.
A. Only in Christ is there hope of a renewal of life.
1. In our earthly bodies we see sin, decay, decomposition and death."
a. "In Adam all die."
b. "The wages of sin is death."
2. In Christ we see the "quickening, life giving Spirit." John 5:21
a. He has overcome death with life eternal.
b. Through obedience to Christ, God gives man everlasting life. John 6:47; 11:25-26; I John 2:25; 5:11-13
It is life from God as it was in Gen. 2:7
3. Jesus is ever ready to give glorious immortality to lost and dying mortal man.
1. He came "that we might have life, and have it more abundantly."
b. Every poor dying soul should be interested in the source of life eternal, Christ the Lord.

III. WE SEE IN CHRIST THE SUPREME LAW.

A. Every man is under law; law of the Gentile before Christ, the Law given by Moses and the prophets, or under law to Christ. I Cor. 9:21.

1. "To be or not to be" is not the question here, but rather, "Which law will I voluntarily come under?"

a. We can choose the law that brought only death, or we can choose the divine law that brings life and true righteousness.

b. We must choose which one; there is no anarchy.

c. Every day, by free moral choice we are choosing whom we will serve, sin unto death, or righteousness unto salvation. Rom. 6:16

B. All holy law is under His authority.

1. We owe Him our unreserved allegiance.

2. No man made law is superior to His.

3. Obedience to Him brings life, and disobedience brings death.

IV. WE SEE IN CHRIST A RESTING PLACE FOR OUR SOUL.

A. He is the "Lord of peace." II Thess. 3:16

1. Men, generally speaking, are looking for peace where no man has ever found it.
Things of earth do not satisfy.

2. True peace and rest are found only in Christ Jesus.
One glimpse of Him would empty the "Psycho-cots" all over this land and make many homes fit to live in again.

3. True rest is not that of torpor, but that of harmony.
With Christ at the controls of our lives, we can meet troubles and victoriously conquer them.

Once in a dream a man was haunted and thwarted by a mysterious veiled figure. As soon as he gained a fortune, this figure snatched it away. When he was about to enter into peace and rest, the veiled figure would attack his mind with fear and anxiety. When he was hungry, that veiled figure would come and take away his food and drink. When he was overcome with weariness and lay down to sleep, this veiled enemy would fill his mind with thoughts that drove sleep from him. When he had won fame, this veiled figure would steal his reputation. When he was at the open door of opportunity, this veiled ghost woud snatch it away. When he stood at the marriage altar, and was about to make his sacred vow, that veiled figure came forward and led away his bride.

He was angry and cried out to his adversary, "Who are you?" Without waiting for the answer, he stretched forth his hand and jerked off the veil of his tormentor. To his amazement the face was his own.

Only when Christ takes the place of SELF can we find peace and victory!

"DO IT YOURSELF. . .EXAMINATION"

I Corinthians 11:28

INTRODUCTION:

This examination requires the utmost care and faithfulness realize that it is of great importance for time and eternity. It is a duty that is sadly neglected. Agreater regard for it would bring more individual holiness and happiness, and less formalism and apathy in the church. Just as inventories are necessary to keep a business on a paying basis, so self-examination makes living for Christ more profitable to God and man.

PROPOSITION: *"Let a man examine himself."*

I. GOD DEMANDS IT. "EXAMINE HIMSELF."
  A. To examine means to inspect, to bring to trial, to make inquiry, for the purpose of truly knowing our hearts.
    1. We are exhorted to "Prove ourselves," to try ourselves as men try metals.
      a. If they are found pure, they are approved and used; but if they are proven impure, they are rejected and counted as reprobate. Jere. 6:29-30
      b. This duty begins at home, where the trials are more wearing.
        (1) It is not an examination of the other person where we are apt to be more censorous.
        (2) We are to look for the beam in our own eye and not the mote in our neighbor's.
    2. We are to examine ourselves as to our acceptance before God.
      a. Are we convinced we were lost, helpless and hopeless?
      b. Has Christ become our Saviour, reconciling us to God?

c. Have we ever rejoiced in His pardoning love and justifying grace?

3. We must examine ourselves as to our faith.
   a. Do we really believe the teaching of the Bible? Can we say truthfully, "I have been crucified with Christ?" Gal. 2:20
   b. Does our faith bear fruit? Jas. 2:14 How are our works?
4. We must examine ourselves as to our hope .
   a. If our faith is right, our hope will be right. Heb. 11:1
   b. Does our faith bear us up in times of trouble?
   c. Does our faith make us dead to the world?
5. We must examine ourselves in connection with Christ's church.
   a. Have we made the church better by our presence?
   b. Are we an honor to it, or do we impede its progress?
   c. Do we desire, seek, pray for, and contribute to its ongoing?
6. We must examine ourselves as to our behavior in the world.
   a. Are we separated unto God, or do we conform to the world? Rom. 12:2
   b. Are we shining lights in it? Do we seek its salvation?

II. HOW SHOULD WE EXAMINE OURSELVES?

A. It should be with solemnity, because it concerns our life here, and in the hereafter.
   1. We should compare our life with the standards God has given.
   2. We should be impartial, not excusing our infirmities, nor apologizing on account of our circumstances. We should examine ourselves as though we were in the presence of God.
   3. We should examine ourselves frequently.
      a. Make every sermon apply to ourselves.
      b. Close every day with an examination, because we may never see the new day.
      c. Before partaking of the Lord's supper, vs. 28b "...and so let him eat of that bread, and drink of that cup."
   4. We should examine ourselves prayerfully.
      a. David prayed, "Search me, O God," Psa. 139:23-24. Let God look into your heart.
      b. Pray for forgiveness, strength, faith and power to glorify God.

B. What is the profit of a true self examination?

1. It shows us where we need to improve, adds to our rewards and general felicity.
2. It helps us not to err, makes us watchful and faithful to duty.
3. It will lead us to become more humble, to repent, to grow in faith, and to a more healthy spiritual state.
4. It will warn us of danger, and lead us to our safe deliverance.

A lookout is on duty at all hours on a ship. If there is any doubt as to the depth of the channel, a trusted seaman is ordered to "heave the lead," and measure the depth. The officer of the deck keeps a close observation and makes repairs immediately before a storm. So we should be in "our ship" on the voyage of life. We do not want to make shipwreck of our lives, so we must examine ourselves daily, being watchful and diligent, looking into our own heart and guarding from anything that would impede our progress. II Cor. 13:5

By a continued examination we are prepared for death. It gives us confidence in our hope of a prosperous eternity with the School Master of our souls, who will give the final examination.

This message is a warning. Don't go on sailing in dangerous conditions any longer. Be warned! Head for port! Don't risk your life and the lives of others by disobeying God.

Newport Beach, California recently reported one of the worst sea tragedies since 1952. A twenty-five foot cabin cruiser with nine anxious occupants had embarked on a fishing expedition. The happy anticipation of fishing was soon shattered, and tragedy electrified everyone as the cruiser sank in the choppy, shark infested waters. When they were found they were all mangled by the sharks. The pieces of bodies had to be fished out of the sea. Sympathetically, we say, "how tragic," but more than this, we are shocked when we learn that the Coast Guard had posted a small craft warning, advising of rough seas with winds up to thirty miles an hour. An official said, "A boat that size would bounce around like a cork." It was all so uncalled for, because they had been warned.

Men have been warned since the days of Adam and Eve. Some have heeded and examined themselves. They listened to the call of God, came to repentance, and found forgiveness in Christ. The power of God made them fit for this world and eternity. Why don't you do that NOW?

"WHAT CAN KEEP US FROM OBSERVING THE COMMUNION?"

I Cor. 10:21 + I Cor. 11:17-22

INTRODUCTION:

The most holy relationships on earth can become unholy and illegal by perversion. God gave this supper to bless us, but these Corinthians were using a blessing to curse themselves. They were not content with what God had given them as a memorial, but they added to it the "love feast." This was a feast in which each one contributed to the "pot luck" affair. This divided the church into castes and cliques causing the rich to despise the poor and the poor to hate the rich. Some became gluttons and drunkards in the presence of those who were hungry and thirsty. Under the circumstances described, Paul said it is impossible for them to eat the Lord's supper.

PROPOSITION: *Some of the things that can keep us from correctly observing the Lord's Supper.*

I. ARROGANCE, HAUGHTINESS AND SELF-CONCEIT.
   A. There is no place for self-approbation or despising one another at the Lord's table.
      1. Pride is always condemned of God.... Prov. 6:16-17; 16:5.
         a. Here it is a glaring sin at a time when men should be humble.
            (1) Communion commemorates Christ's death for our sins, bankrupt sinners that we are.
            (2) Certainly there is no room for pride. Mk. 10:45
         b. It is absurd to think of a proud person rightly partaking of the Lord's Supper, no one should attempt it with such a heart. Jas. 4:6
      2. In humility we should remember how vile we were and how pure was the One who gave His life for us. I Cor. 11:24
         a. We should generously forgive all who have sinned against us, even as He forgave us our sins. Eph. 4:32
         b. We should despise ourselves for our sinfulness that caused the "Lamb of God" to be sacrificed. I Tim. 1:15

II. THOUGHTLESSNESS OF THE COST OF THE SACRIFICE.

A. This was the cause of the actions of the Corinthians.

1. It made them act irreverently, despising Him who died for them.
2. Thoughtlessness today can come into our lives as we sit at the table of the Lord. (God forbid that it ever should)

   Reading the Sunday school papers, writing and reading notes, fixing our hair, and whispering, proclaim immediately our inability to partake of the Communion acceptably.
3. Every Christian should be filled with awe as we remember the justice of God in this death, and the mercy of God in this memorial. It was for us! Rom. 3:23-26

III. ALIENATION AND DISUNITY.

A. Christians are to be of the same mind and judgment. (I Cor. 1:10) and this is especially so at the Lord's supper. I Cor. 10:17

   If we come to the table hating and despising one another, we are breaking the greatest commandment, while we profess to keep a memorial to love and unity. John 13:34

   a. The God who loved us in our sinfulness and the Christ who gave His life for sinners, must be terribly offended when He sees His ransomed people in such a condition.
   b. The only way we can be ONE with Christ is to be ONE with His family, the church, the household of God. Eph. 2:19; I Tim. 3:15

B. The communion memorial commemorates the death of Christ for all our sins.

   It brings us back to God and at peace with each other, making even Jews and Gentiles ONE body.

IV. GLUTTONY AND DRUNKENNESS.

A. These two sins have been the curse of mankind in every age of prosperity. Luke 21:34

1. Some people come to love their "food and drink" more than they love their brothers in Christ. Rom. 14:14-23
2. Knowing that the drunkard shall not enter heaven, how could these professed Christians indulge in deliberate sin at the Holy Communion? I Cor. 6:10

   a. The devil blinded their eyes.
   b. They ate before the others arrived, thus showing they were unfit for the Spiritual feast.

c. Indulgence in alcoholic beverages either before the communion, during it, or after, advertises a sinful heart in rebellion against the Lord.
   (1) Both religious and irreligious men have sought some excuse for their drinking. We are just as drunk as the amount we drink; just as a thief is a thief no matter what amount he steals. One penny marks a man a thief.
   (2) It is easy for a sinner to rationalize and excuse his actions, but here Paul leaves no loophole.

Today we have become so involved in "how often" we are to keep the Lord's Supper, that we have forgotten the importance of the manner in which we are to observe it. Paul emphasized the latter here.

Young converts sometimes teach old "dead heads" some of the first principles of Christianity. A new convert in an African mission was sitting one Sunday at the communion table. He looked across the room and his face filled with hatred, malice and a burning desire for revenge. He got up and rushed out of the assembly. After some time he returned to his place at the table where he sat in humble, calm reverence and devotion.

Afterward he was questioned as to his behaviour. He explained that the person he saw was the pagan who had killed his father and whom he had sworn to kill for revenge. He had gone out by himself and asked God for help... Remembering that Christ died for him, and that it was his own sins that crucified Christ, could he come in and partake of the Communion in a manner pleasing to God, forgiving his enemy. Paul's lesson is an eternal lesson for all Christians.

"NOW CONCERNING THE SPIRITUAL GIFTS"

I Corinthians 12:1-11

INTRODUCTION:

It is well to remember when dealing with the subject of Spiritual gifts in the early church, that they had no New Testament to preach or refer to as authoritative. They had to have something to prove their message was divine. Hebrews 2:3-4 tells us that these men were equipped with miraculous power for the purpose of confirming their message. They had what we do not have, miraculous Spiritual gifts; we have what they did not have, the complete and authenticated New Covenant. They knew in part but we know all of the revelation God gave to men.

PROPOSITION: *Important thoughts about the Spiritual gifts in Corinth.*

I. THEIR COMING WAS PROPHESIED.

A. Peter quoted Joel 2:28 in connection with the manifestation of the Holy Spirit on Pentecost.

B. Christ gave, in connection with the Great Commission, the promise of miraculous power to His Apostles. Mark 16:17-18

Connecting this prophecy with Heb. 2:3-4 we have the reason WHY they were given, and how they were used.

C. How else could a supernatural message be established except by supernatural demonstrations?

1. The Lord they preached was a wonderful miracle Himself.
2. His life was filled with the miraculous as He established His Deity. John 20:30-31

II. THE FIELD THEY COVERED WAS WIDE AND VARIOUS.

A. There are nine specific gifts mentioned in this chapter.

1. They are: wisdom, knowledge, faith, healing, miracles, prophecy, discerning spirits, tongues, and the interpretation of tongues. Vss. 8-10

God in His omniscience gave just the gifts needed.

B. He knew how wide the field would be to which He could appeal in the miraculous.

The century that followed the establishment of the church proves His divine wisdom.

C. In nature, one member supplements the other, so each of these gifts supplemented the others, thus making a complete, efficient, functioning body.

III. THE PURPOSE OF THE SPIRITUAL GIFTS.

A. Negatively stated:

1. They were not for the personal agrandizement of the miracle worker.

Simon, the sorcerer, seemed to desire them for that purpose and he was rebuked severely. Acts 8:18-24

B. Positively stated:

1. They were to guide the church because they had no Holy Spirit inspired word to guide them.
2. They were to strengthen the faith of those new converts who would be tempted constantly to turn back.
3. They would appeal to the unbeliever as a basis for believing the divine message. (special equipment for a special mission)
4. They were given to glorify God.

   Their source was God, therefore the result would be to glorify the source!
5. They established "The Church of the Living God," in contrast to the dead, powerless idols.

C. They were used with reverence as in His presence.

1. We can receive "The gift of the Holy Spirit" (Acts 2:38) that will change our lives completely.

   We should use the indwelling presence of the Holy Spirit in our lives to glorify God just as they used their miraculous spiritual gifts to glorify Him. Eph. 4:8-13
2. We must use our gifts carefully.

   A good gift carelessly used could do as much harm as it was intended to do good.
3. We must remember He demands an accounting of the gifts He entrusts to us. Matt. 25:19-30

   Although each gift is from God, the responsibility for the use of it rests on us!

IV. GOD IS THE DISTRIBUTOR.

A. We should not grumble at the gift we receive or be jealous of the gifts of others, for that would be judging God.

1. We must realize we are but mortals, and He is the eternal God.

   It behooves us not to grumble at the gift or gifts He has given us, or to compare our gifts with others.

B. We should use our God-given talents to the best of our abilities, in order to return a profit to Him who gave.

1. God demands a reckoning from us just the same as He demanded a reckoning from the early miraculously endowed Christians.

   Let us be worthy of the term, "Good servants.'

On the Isle of Man there is an old stone tower covered with ivy, where one of the best governors the isle ever had was hung.

He had been accused of treachery and imprisoned. Intercession had been made and he had been vindicated and his pardon sent to the jailor. Somehow the pardon fell into the hands of his enemies and the good governor was hung. Now there is a pathetic ballad sung to the memory of this good man.

We are horror-struck when we think of a man who has been pardoned hung as a traitor. But let us be careful how we despise that ungodly man, especially if we have not used our God-given gifts to carry the message of pardon to all sinners on the earth. God may some day say, "Thou art the man! You had the pardon in your hand to save the condemned man from eternal death." We have God's gift, heaven given ability to tell some one about Christ. God will hold us accountable for the use of it, just as he did the early Christians for the use of the miraculous spiritual gifts.

"THE BODY OF CHRIST, THE CHURCH"

I Corinthians 12:12-27

INTRODUCTION:

By inspiration the Apostle chose to represent the church as a "body" right in the midst of disunity and quarreling. What a clear picture of the unity and order that should exist in the church! What is more united yet varied, more organized and yet more independent then the physical body and the Lord's church? Both the body and the church have one head and many members acting individually, but all for the good of the whole. The emphasis here is upon the members of the body instead of the Head. There is no disunity in the Head; disunity is always in the workings of the members.

PROPOSITION: *How the name "The body of Christ" fits the church.*

I. THE BODY CONSISTS OF MANY AND VARIED MEMBERS. Vss. 12-20
   A. Because the members are not all the same, this makes for beauty.
      1. We are by nature lovers of variety as it blends into beauty.

2. The church has different sizes, shapes, ages, and abilities.
   a. Every member differs from the other, and yet they are all part of the body. Vs. 15
3. Sometimes there are too many "chiefs" and not enough "indians," (or vice versa) but God has seen to it that, generally speaking, the church is well balanced.
   We all have our own place of suitable work.
4. We are all baptized into <u>One</u> body and God puts us in our respective places of service. Vs. 18

II. THERE ARE MANY DUTIES TO BE PERFORMED IN THE BODY. Vss. 21-24

A. Somewhere along the line there is a place of service for everyone.
   1. As in the physical body, each member has a task to perform peculiar to itself; so in the church each member has his own duty to perform.
      No one can take his place successfully.
   2. There are no inferior members.
      The eye can not do the work of a toe, and the toe is not inferior if it does its work, so in the church each member has his duty and he MUST do it.

III. IN A BODY EVERY MEMBER IS UNITED TO EVERY OTHER MEMBER.

A. Amputated members are useless to the body, for only as the members are united and working harmoniously can the body function properly.
   1. So it should be in the church, the body of Christ.
      a. Every member is dependent upon every other member.
      b. The church is not like a landscape with a lake here, a tree there, and a rock over yonder, it is all united.
   2. We are under the Headship of Christ, therefore we are in vital union with every other baptized believer in the body.
   3. The idea of an "up-town church" and a "skid-row" mission should be out.
      If both groups are born-again children of God, they are all in ONE body; no member isolates himself from any other member or members.

4. The member who refuses to have anything to do with the other members has "amputated himself" from the body. (He is soon dead)
5. John asks, "How can a man love God whom he has not seen, if he cannot love His children whom he has seen?" cf. John 13:34
6. Christians are dependent upon each other, not separate.
   a. United, we are the body of Christ, not individually!
   b. We are helped by others and we are to help others.
   c. It takes bass, tenor, and alto singers in a choir as well as sopranos, to make complete harmony.

IV. ALL MEMBERS ARE NOT OF EQUAL IMPORTANCE.

A. It is not always the most comely parts of the body that are of the most vital importance. Vss. 23-24
   1. One can get along without hair, teeth, ears, or eyes, but his liver is an essential, unseen but very important.
   2. The "tongues" gift showed off well, but Paul says, "yet shew I unto you a more excellent way." (Chapter 13)
      There are things more excellent than the showy gifts in the church.
   3. The strong appearing legs or arms are not so important as the nerves that keep our respiratory system functioning.
      So in the church, the most important members may not be the most prominent ones.
   4. Every member in the body is important and in the church every member is important.
      a. Strong members should protect the weaker members.
      b. The hands and shoulders are used by a fighter to protect his eyes, so let the church members who are strong help the weak members.

V. IN THE BODY THERE IS UNITY AND AT THE SAME TIME GREAT DIVERSITY. Vs. 20

A. The life in the blood pervades the entire human body or it is dead.
   1. In the church the life from God is in every member, or they are dead!
      a. They cooperate to make the body function.
      b. It is one family, made alive by one Spirit, partaking of one loaf and advancing one cause.

2. The eternal life, given by God to every member, fills every member of the body causing them to move in a Godly way.
   a. This causes mutual sympathy among the members and as one member of the body suffers all the others suffer with it.

VI. THE BODY IS UNDER ONE HEAD. Eph. 1:22-23
  A. The body may live with some of its members amputated.
    1. Sometimes gangrenous members must be cut off, but it is impossible for the body to live if it is severed from the Head, physically or spiritually.
       There must be a vital connection with Christ, or death ensues!
    2. When St. Vitus's dance attacks a body, the members do not obey the head, and the body becomes a grotesque figure and practically useless.
       a. So it is in the church; the HEAD must give the orders!
       b. We must obey if there is to be retained the semblance of a "body."
    3. Disorderly members cause the "body of Christ," the church, to be evil spoken of. II Thess. 3:6; 11-14

How do we get into the body of Christ? Gal. 3:26-27 makes it clear that we are baptized into Christ; we put on Christ, and we begin to function as members of His Body, the church. He adds those who are saved to the church. Acts 2:38-47 Why not accept Him, now, brother? Become a member of His Body now!

"THE EXCELLENCY OF CHRISTIAN LOVE MUST BE EXHIBITED"

I Corinthians 13:1-7

INTRODUCTION:

This love is not the love exhibited between two members of the opposite sex; it is not merely "charity" or "alms-giving," it is the mutual feelings of persons endowed with the same Spiritual nature. It is a sentiment which governs the lovers actions or conduct, restraining them from any harmful action and stimulating them to go beyond duty to assist the person loved.

PROPOSITION: *How is this love manifest?*

I. IT IS SUPERIOR TO SPEECH. Vs. 1
   A. It seems as though the gift of tongues or speech, was the highest prize for which the Corinthians were striving.
      1. Tongues centered peoples mind on the speaker, while love covered up the giver and helped the needy.
      2. Love is far more important to the church than mere exhibitions of the "tongues movement."
         Love makes us take a child to rear, help the weak, minister to the sick, give to the poor, and comfort those who sorrow.

II. LOVE IS SUPERIOR TO KNOWLEDGE. Vs. 2a
   A. The great gifts of prophecy, understanding of mysteries, and knowledge would make a strong appeal to Corinthians, but Paul places love above any of them.
      1. Speaking forth the mind of God by direct knowledge is wonderful.
         It would appeal to the "intellectuals," but love surpasses it in importance; love is a "better way."
      2. Knowledge can be useless to the possessor if he has not love.
         "Knowledge puffeth up, but love edifieth." I Cor. 8:1b
      3. One can be a great speaker, have endless knowledge from books, great teaching power, but without love he is nothing.
         Love infuses the spirit in which the knowledge should be infused; it controls the purpose of teaching.

III. LOVE IS SUPERIOR TO FAITH. Vs. 2b
   A. Paul was the great preacher of faith, so he is not disparaging faith, merely putting it in its proper place.
      1. Faith must come into the heart before Christian love can come in, because we become children of God through faith. Gal. 3:26
         a. When one is in Christ, the Holy Spirit produces love in his life.
         b. We love Him because He first loves us, and then we love our fellowmen, to be like our Saviour.
      2. Gifts are not always a sign of piety, but love always is.
         a. Removing mountains would be a miracle and apparently some of these folk had miraculous power but NO love!

b. Remember Paul had both the LOVE OF GOD and all of these supernatural gifts, so he could compare them honestly and from experience.

IV. LOVE IS SUPERIOR TO ALMS-GIVING. Vs. 3a

A. We associate giving with love, but one can give merely to be seen of men or to make a big name for himself.

1. Some people give merely because it is the custom of their church to give a certain amount.

a. Rockefeller used to give each of his caddies a dime, but no one would intimate that he loved the hard working little fellows who carried his clubs.

b. Some big men and corporations give bountifully during an election year to the fund of their candidate, not because they love the man; but because they want some favor and this is the manner by which they attain it.

V. LOVE IS SUPERIOR TO MARTYRDOM. Vs. 3b

A. Many persons can suffer physical harm and not flinch. I am not belittling those who have died for Christ, but unless the martyr dies because he loves, it is a sacrifice that gains nothing.

a. Self-glorification came into prominence during the great persecutions and many sought martyrdom for martyrdom's sake.

b. Self can have an awful hold on people, even leading them to give their lives, but God knows who it is they love.

VI. HOW DOES LOVE CAUSE US TO BEHAVE? Vss. 4-5

A. Love suffers long, is not impatient.

1. Love has no ill will or malice, but is gracious and kind. The conduct of others should not turn our love into hate.

B. Love shuts out envy and jealousy.

Love forgets the evil others have done and tries to put the best interpretation on others actions.

C. Love puts down selfish pride.

1. Love does not make men boasters. "Vaunteth not itself."

2. Love makes men humble. "Is not puffed up."

D. If we are loving and thinking of others, the desire to make ourselves appear big, will be taken away from us.
   1. It will make us behave ourselves "Seemly."
   2. Love is unselfish, "Seeketh not its own." Vs. 5

Love was the remedy for all the defects in Corinth. It brought harmony where there was division, order where there was disorder, and correction of all misuses. Christians should always seek to excel in this greatest of gifts. Love will cause us to walk in the way of life which transcends all others. Paul so excelled and so walked. He said, "follow me, as I follow the Lord."

Love is brought into our lives by the Holy Spirit. It is as boundless as the ocean. God grant that you will become a Christian, and be given new life from the Father.

"COSMOLOGICAL DEITY"

I Corinthians 14:33

INTRODUCTION:

Cosmos is the opposite of chaos. All was chaos when God began to form the earth into an habitation for man. When He finished there was order. When the devil came into the affairs of men there was disorder again. God is not the God of confusion, but of peace, and order.

This text has its setting in Corinth right where the devil had been causing all manner of disorder and confusion. Women were out of their place, the tongue craze had swept over them, and often there was no interpreter to make any sense out of what was spoken. This confusion Paul condemned as a spokesman for God.

PROPOSITION: *How is God shown to be a God of order?*

I. THE PROCESS OF CREATION FROM THE FIRST DAY THROUGH THE SIXTH EXHIBITS A GOD OF ORDER AND DESIGN. Gen. chp. 1 and 2.
   A. Each step in the order of creation is a natural development making ready for that which was to follow.
      1. God did not get the fish here before He had the ocean, nor plants before He had land, water and sun.

B. From the first experiments of scientists, they have depended upon the "laws of nature."
   1. God made those laws.
   2. There is uniformity of action under the same conditions.
   3. Where there is law there must be a law given.
      Plans demand a planner.
   4. We can depend on the sun to make its orbit, the earth to turn regularly on its axis, and seasons that come regularly.
   5. We can depend on the laws of conception and birth in breeding.
      a. Chickens do not bring forth colts.
      b. God is the God of cosmological order.

II. THE PLAN OF REDEMPTION AS DEVELOPED THROUGH THE CENTURIES IS ORDERLY.
   A. God dealt with individuals when the family was the unit.
      Fathers were prophets, priests, kings and military leaders.
   B. When men became numerous, God united them into a nation, giving them laws to maintain a well ordered nation. Ex. 20; and Lev. 20.
      When greater numbers of sacrifices needed to be made, He set aside a priesthood for that purpose, with orderly services and rituals. (Leviticus)
   C. In the "fulness of time," when the world had shown its inability to save itself, God sent forth His Son.
      1. His coming had been foretold for centuries.
         In the orderly fulfillment, He made His debut. Gal. 4:4-6
      2. His deity was established by showing that He had power over the laws of nature. John 3:1-3
         He changed the water into wine.
      3. This culminated in the fulfillment of God's plan of the ages to bring in a sacrifice for man that would make him a fit companion for God, again.
         a. He came to seek and to save the lost, according to God's plan.
         b. He offered Himself; He died, was buried, and rose from the dead to prove He was able to save us and to give us a demonstration of His power over the grave.

c. God never got ahead of Himself; He kept the redemption plan unfolding in order.

When Jesus found things out of order in the temple, He set things in order in a Godly manner. Jno. 2:13-17

III. THE BEGINNING AND DEVELOPMENT OF THE CHURCH IS IN AN ORDERLY MANNER.

A. As Pentecost commemorated the giving of the old law, so God chose that day to begin the new dispensation.

1. Three thousand persons died at the giving of the old law; 3,000 were saved at the giving of the new.
2. A great manifestation of the power of God preceded the preaching of the new message of salvation. Acts 2:1-6
3. The means of salvation was preached before the offer of salvation was made. Acts 2:36-37
4. Sin was condemned before sinners were commanded to repent of their sins. Acts 2:23
5. Christ's resurrection was preached before the offer of resurrection was made to sinners. Acts 2:31
6. The Holy Spirit was poured upon the obedient and chosen Apostles before it was offered to the obedient disciples. Acts 2:1; Acts 2:38
7. Christ had ascended (Acts 1:9) before the hope of our ascension to meet Him in the air was preached. (I Thess. 4:17)
8. He is preparing us a place before we are invited to that place. John chp. 14
9. Gospel preachers were sent out with good news, only after the demonstration of God's power had been given on which to base their message.
10. Everything is ready now, the Spirit and the Bride say, "Come."

"All things are ready, come to the feast,
Come for the table now is spread."

God has put order in our salvation. The order is go preach the gospel; this is followed by the sinner hearing the message and believing it. Next comes the demand for genuine repentance from sin, and obedience in baptism in the likeness of Christ's death for our sins. It is orderly, and God given, with the promise that He will take away all our sins.

Oh friend, will you believe this great Cosmological Deity as he calls you from ruin to salvation by the way of the Cross? It is open to all who will come to God by Him. Come while the call is clear and you have ability to respond. No man knows the day nor the hour when the last call will come.

"LET HIM BE ADVERTISED AS A FOOL"

I Corinthians 14:37-38

INTRODUCTION:

In verse 37 Paul lays claim to inspiration in the things he was writing to them. "They are the commandments of the Lord." And in verse 38 states that if any person did not recognize his writings as inspired of God, then he was ignorant and not worthy of further attention; it was wilful ignorance.

Paul did not elevate himself, but he did magnify his office as a Holy Spirit inspired Apostle of Christ. Personally, he said he was less than the least of the followers of Christ, but as an Apostle he was equal with the greatest, meeting in open combat the apostle from Jerusalem, Peter. Gal. 2:14

When Paul wrote these words (V 37-38) he knew there would be those who would challenge him, men who accepted no authority except their own intellects. Paul had met them, and knew of their existence in Corinth, so he gave his judgment on them in righteous indignation.

PROPOSITION: *Why should these defectors be looked upon as ignorant?*

I. IF THEY REJECTED THIS INSPIRED MESSAGE, THEY WERE EITHER NOT INSPIRED OR WERE WILFULLY MISLEADING OTHERS THROUGH THEIR OPINIONS.
   A. Strongly opinionated individuals are often just plain ignorant.
      Working in many churches has convinced me that those who are dead-set on keeping something that is merely an opinion, are not the most level-headed people.
      a. People of this nature will resist the most evident truths, and thereby advertise their lack of sound judgment.

b. Prejudice makes men blind to that which any unprejudiced person can see readily.

B. If the evidence Paul presented was not enough to convince the skeptical, then they would not be convinced by anything.
1. Some people will not be convinced.
No authority appeals to them except their own opinions.
2. There are those who will not live by reason, laws of society, or act in a candid or dispassionate manner.
a. Paul referred to some as "dogs." Philippians 3:2
b. Jesus referred to some others as "sons of the Devil." John 8:44
c. In their finality they killed prophets, delivered up Christ, and forbade preaching the gospel. I Thess. 2:14-17
3. One does not have to preach very long to find out that there are those who are "enemies of the cross of Christ."
a. They will not believe the truth, but seek only their own glory.
b. They seek to obscure the truth by their own ignorance and maliciousness.

II. SOMETIMES IN AN EFFORT TO REACH THEM SO MUCH ATTENTION IS GIVEN TO THEM THAT THEY RECEIVE MORE PUBLICITY AND DRAW MORE FOLLOWERS THAN IF THEY HAD BEEN LEFT ALONE.

A. If they love ignorance and want to walk in the dark, it is impossible to reach them. They are the opposite of John 7:17.
1. All truly born again people are slow to give any person up, but if they refuse the inspired Word of God, we must.
a. Even God gives some people up. Rom. 1:24-28
(1) God finally gave up on Israel and Judah, and sent them no more prophets, but gave them up to captivity in Assyria and Babylon!
(2) After 120 years of Noah's preaching, God gave up that wicked generation because they refused His inspired prophet.
2. When it is impossible for us to reach them, we should get away from them and pray that they may be saved in God's own manner.

III. ONE SOUL IS JUST AS IMPORTANT TO GOD AS ANOTHER, SO IF WE CAN CONVERT A HUNDRED SOULS WHILE WE WASTE TIME ON ONE DELIBERATELY IGNORANT SINNER, WE ARE NOT GOOD STEWARDS.

A. We should ask God to send us those who have an open mind to receive His truth.

1. In such people we know the sowing of the seed will bring forth a worthy crop.

Of the wilfully ignorant Jesus said, "Cast not your pearls before swine."

2. Why plow rocks when the world is waiting for the plow to be used on rich fields of earnest people?

We should find good soil and sow in it, or we waste our lives.

IV. WHEN OPINIONATED AND IGNORANT MEN REFUSE THE TRUTH, THEY MUST BE TURNED OVER TO THE GOD OF JUDGMENT, WHO WILL SPEAK IN "THE GREAT DAY OF VISITATION."

A. Our message must be willingly accepted; we are not policemen, nor an army to force people to accept it.

1. Roman Catholicism and Mohammedanism have made converts in that way.
2. Jesus told His disciples in certain instances to "shake off the dust of your feet" and depart. Matt. 10:14
3. Paul practiced what he preached in Acts 13:50-51; Acts 14:20; Acts 17:32-33.

When the Word of God is preached to men and they refuse to hearken time after time and rebel against it, we must turn away from them by Divine injunction.

Opinionated sinners are like the skeptic in Galileo's day. Galileo invented a telescope with which he observed the satellites of Jupiter, and invited a man who was opposed to him to look through it that he might be convinced. The man refused, saying, "If I should see them how could I maintain my opinions which I have advanced against your teaching." So he refused to look. He determined to remain ignorant.

The work of God that has convicted millions of people, from childhood to the greatest thinkers, is not to be shunted aside without having to answer to God. The Gospel it presents is medicine that will give life forever; if it is refused it will bring death forever. Be careful how you choose when you hear the Word preached.

"THE GREATEST TREATISE ON THE RESURRECTION"

I Corinthians 15:1-58

INTRODUCTION:

This chapter is actually complete in itself, although a part of the general epistle. This is the theology of the resurrection, dealing in reason, eloquence and a spiritual treatment of the subject. Paul contends that the resurrection of Christ is the basis and foundation of the entire Christian faith. He meets the opposition in Corinth, typical of all opponents to this doctrine, with logic and revelation. Paul gives hope to wavering humanity when he said immortality is certain to be received because Christ has been raised from the dead, victor over the grave; whereby He offers immortality to all those who believe on Him.

PROPOSITION: *Doctrine of the Resurrection.*

I. FIRST, HE PROVES CHRIST'S RESURRECTION. Vss. 1-11
   A. It is basic to Christian preaching. Vs. 2
      1. It is based upon fulfilled prophecies from the Old Testament. Psa. 16:8 ff and Psa. 110:1
      2. All the Apostles and the 500 are proof of His being alive after His death. Vss. 4-7
      3. Paul adds his own testimony in its true setting. Vss. 9-11
         By this time the gospel message had been preached and accepted in all the churches in the world. Col. 1:6

II. NEXT HE INFERS FROM THIS CERTAIN FACTS. Vss. 12-28
   A. He shows how the facts of the gospel defeat the false doctrines being preached in Corinth.
      They were saying the dead do not rise.
   B. He follows this by affirming that Christ is risen and that all true believers are to rise. Vss. 20-28
      1. He is the "first fruits." Vs. 20 + I Tim. 6:16
      2. He is the resurrection. Vs. 21
      3. He is the life-giver. Vs. 22
      4. He is the one who will deliver up the "Living Kingdom" to God. Vss. 24-26
      5. Christ is in subjection ONLY to God. Vss. 27-28

III. HE AFFIRMS THAT THE WILLING MARTYRDOM OF THE FOLLOWERS OF CHRIST IS EVIDENCE OF THEIR FAITH IN THE RESURRECTION. Vss. 29-49

A. Christians were being opposed, ridiculed, persecuted, and killed for their faith in the risen Christ.

This new doctrine, demonstrated by the risen Christ, made new creatures out of men who before feared death. Vss. 29-33

B. He appeals to natural phenomena to illustrate life after death.

1. He draws from a common practice, the planting of a seed and the new form of life it produces after its death. Vss. 35-38
2. If God can make and has made different varieties of flesh, we can trust Him to give us a NEW body after the resurrection. Vss. 39-41
3. The same God who made a body for Adam, can make a new body for the "Second Adam." Vss. 42-49

IV. HE AFFIRMS THAT THERE ARE SOME THINGS WE CANNOT UNDERSTAND FULLY ABOUT THIS PROCESS. Vss. 50-57

A. He states that flesh and blood cannot inherit this kingdom. Vs. 50

1. He tells them a mystery. Vss. 50-53
2. He informs them that victory is complete after the resurrection, and the giving of the immortal body. Vs. 54
3. Then we can sing and shout a new victory cry. Vs. 55
4. In this ecstasy we must remember that sin is the sting of death, and that Christ has freed us from it. Vss. 56-57
    a. From prehistoric times men have feared sin and death along with a natural retribution from the just judge.
    b. This is removed by a propitiatory sacrifice, suffered vicariously by the Lamb of God, our redeemer and Saviour.

V. HE TERMINATES THE DISCUSSION WITH AN EARNEST EXHORTATION TO FAITHFULNESS UNTO DEATH. Vs. 58

A. They were not to be lazy, but "abounding."

1. They should not be self-confident; it was "The Lord's doing."
2. They were to be mindful that they labored for the Lord, who knows hearts, faith and conduct.

3. They were to live in constant hope of life forever granted by the Eternal God, who raised up His Son and promised eternal life to all true believers. John 3:36

Dr. Hinson made the following statement one year after his case had been diagnosed as incurable and the illness which brought his death one year later. "I remember a year ago when the doctor said I was dying. I walked to my home, five miles from the city, and I looked at the mountain that I love, and at the river in which I rejoice, and at the stately trees that are poetry to my soul. In the evening I looked up into the great sky where God was lighting His evening lamps, and I said: 'I may not see you many more times, mountain, but I shall be alive when you are gone; and river, I shall be alive when you have ceased running toward the sea; and stars, I shall be alive when you have fallen from your sockets in the great down-pulling of the material universe.'"

That was the confidence one man had in Christ, the risen Lord. It can be your steadfast hope and secure trust. Is it yours? Why not make it yours today?

"THE COLLECTION FOR THE SAINTS"

I Corinthians 16:1-5

INTRODUCTION:

This was not only a collection for the saints, but also a collection from the saints. On the very day the Lord rose from the dead and came forth to tell of His victory, they were to take up their collections and put them in a special storehouse. This was added to each week until Paul and his helpers came to carry it to Jerusalem to succor the poor saints there. It was to be set apart, added to regularly, and kept in a storehouse for relief funds. In this one act they practised many Christian virtues. They were educating the hand, purse, and soul. God was prospering them so they in turn could help others of less fortunate circumstances. They were to give it cheerfully, habitually, and in a business like manner. This would help break down the wall between Gentile and Jew as these Gentiles assisted the Jews in Jerusalem.

PROPOSITION: *Outstanding features about this collection.*

I. IT WAS PROMOTED BY THE APOSTLE TO THE GENTILES.
  A. He said, "Now concerning the collection for the saints."
    1. He was always a man of intense zeal when there was a need.
    2. It was Paul who reminded us that "It is more blessed to give than.... Acts 20:35.
    3. Wisely, he pits the giving of the Galatians with the giving of the Corinthians.
       The Corinthians are used as an example to the citizens of Macedonia. cf. II Cor. chp. 8 and 9.
    4. This was a wide spread collection for the saints.
       a. It is referred to in Romans 15:26 and II Cor. 9:2 as well as in Acts 11:28-30.
       b. Great need demands great sacrifices.
    5. The earnest urgency of these great men helped to keep alive the spirit of Christian sharing.
       a. Their example has been a blessing to those in every land for centuries.
       b. Certainly this is a living, vital portion of the Christian religion that can be witnesses by the world.

II. THIS WAS NOT A SLIP-SHOD AFFAIR, BUT ONE THAT WAS WELL ORGANIZED AND DIRECTED.
  A. Paul gave orders that would make it personal: "Let every one of you lay by him in store." Vs. 2
    1. Every one was to have a share, rich, poor, young or old.
       What they possessed they were to give; money, food, clothing.
    2. There was to be a system to their contributing.
       a. The very day was set aside by the Apostle. "Upon the first day of the week...."
       b. This was to be continuous.
       c. Their week began in a kindly act of graciousness to others.
    3. Their giving was to remind them of the source of their blessings.
       a. "As God hath prospered him...."
       b. The blessings received determined the amount that was to be given, and must be given to have a clear conscience in that time of terrible famine.

(1) This was a much needed admonition, because usually the more blessings God gives, the less the receiver desires to share.
(2) Often times we look upon the man who gives thousands of dollars as a very generous man, when in reality his proportionate giving may be far below that of others who gave less.

c. In the Old Testament when prosperity came from God, it was often used to worship the devil. Jere. 13:25-27

III. THE COLLECTION, SO CAREFULLY AND RELIGIOUSLY COLLECTED, WAS TO BE JUST AS CAREFULLY TRANSPORTED AND DISTRIBUTED. Vss. 3-4

A. Paul gives his word to this effect. "Whomsoever ye shall approve by your letters, them will I send to bring your liberality unto Jerusalem."

1. We can learn from this that church collections are not to be handled carelessly.
   Every treasurer, for his own sake, should have someone count the money with him and a double record should be kept.
2. Paul was willing, if the need demanded, to go with them to see that the goods were delivered to the proper people.
   a. This would assure the givers that their gifts were being taken care of properly.
   b. It would assure the receivers that this was a genuine gift from Christians who love them and had concern for them.
      (1) It was not just a "handout."
      (2) The Jerusalem Christians were brothers and sisters in distress.

IV. THIS SHOULD HAVE TAUGHT THE CORINTHIANS, AND ALL OTHER GENTILES, THE FICKLENESS OF PROSPERITY.

A. It should have made them realize that they might be the next ones needing help.
B. They should have remembered that it was the Jews that had shared the Gospel with them by sending Paul and Barnabas.
C. If they had shared with them their Spiritual blessings, was it any great matter that they shared with them their material blessings? I Cor. 9:11-12

This Christian giving, in a practical way, should remind us that it was God who gave the greatest example of giving for without the gift of His Son, mankind was forever lost and alienated from God. The same Christ, who gave His life for us, demands that we give ourselves to Him. Mark 10:45; Mark 8:34-38; Luke 14:26-33. All giving in God's sight begins with the giving of ourselves to Him. God demands a complete surrender!

A commander who held a rock fortress in India, surrendered his stronghold to Alexander. Then Alexander made him governor of it and the surrounding country, saying, "I take this for a wise man who chose rather to commit himself to a good man than to a strong fort."

It is the wise man who delivers up himself to the great and wise God. Only then can God give him a place in His kingdom and save him from destruction.

Why not yield to the Lord Jesus today, and let Him bless and keep you against that day?